MANGER MINISTRIES
15306 Stony Oaks Ln
Prather, CA 93651

When Do I Cry Wolf?

By Steven R. Catt

Contact Me At:
steven@stevencattministries.com
www.stevencattministries.com

Copyright © 2009 by Steven R. Catt

When Do I Cry Wolf?
by Steven R. Catt

Printed in the United States of America

ISBN 978-1-60791-194-4

All rights reserved solely by the author. The author guarantees all contents are original and do not infringe upon the legal rights of any other person or work. No part of this book may be reproduced in any form without the permission of the author. The views expressed in this book are not necessarily those of the publisher.

Unless otherwise indicated, Bible quotations are taken from The New American Standard Bible. Copyright © 1960, 1962, 1963, 1968, 1971, 1972, 1973, 1975, 1977, 1995 by The Lockman Foundation.

www.xulonpress.com

.

DEDICATION

Have you ever been discouraged? I have! There was a time when I decided that life in the ministry was too stressful. I had faced the wolf too many times, and my wounds were deep. I had made the decision that I was just going to call it quits, find a church that I could fade into, and simply drop out of sight. It was at that time that I met Steve. He saw something in me that I didn't see in myself. On December 12, 1992, at the lowest point of my life, Steve, his wife, Carolina, and his mother, Alyce, purchased a new motorhome for us. I asked Steve, "Why would you invest in me? I have no ministry." And he replied with a smile, "You will."

For those of you whom the wolf has hunted, and you are not sure that you want to carry on; remember there is someone who believes in you. Jesus said, *"Peter, Satan has desired to sift you like wheat, but I have prayed for you."* Before you make your decision to quit, I want you to remember that someone is praying for you tonight. Someone, somewhere believes in you.

Thank you, Steve, Carolina, and Alyce for believing in me.

Dedicated to the memory of Charles Steven Lindholm.
June 14, 1948 – October 15, 2005

TABLE OF CONTENTS

FORWARD

It is with great honor that I highly recommend *When Do I Cry Wolf*. Steven Catt has blown me away with his wisdom of spiritual authority marked by an unwavering commitment to God's word. I will never forget one of the first conversations I had with Steven and his sweet wife Cathie, when he looked me square in the eye and said "hello apostle, I know who you really are." To this day I am not comfortable with the term used with my name, but I understand that God gives spheres of authority beyond a local church, to see to it that cities are transformed instead of leaders just building churches.

To this day I am both drawn to Steven and also humbled by his teaching, because I was given his book at a time when I was under unprecedented personal attack and could not make sense of it. It is hard to fight a battle when the enemy is from the inside, and after 18 years in ministry I am convinced this type of spiritual warfare is so damaging that most shepherds simply retreat or give up hope in leading a true movement of God. If you are a church leader, paid or unpaid, elder, deacon, or just a committed member of your local church, this book will offer you hope in a battle you may hardly be aware of. If you are a pastor who feels his vision is being hijacked, then stop and thank God for the book you hold in your hands! God has just equipped you with a reference point and level of truth that will fire you up and give you the courage to do what you already know is right, but just needed a leader who oversees and shepherds pastors (dare I say an apostle?) to help you through these difficult times. I must leave you with a warning: you will never look at church the same again, because you now will see the good fight for what it really is: establishing and defending the Kingdom of God so God's people can have dominion over this earth as intended from the beginning. Pray. Read on, prepare on your knees…and lead with diligence!

Bil Cornelius
Founder and Senior Pastor
Bay Area Fellowship, Corpus Christi, Texas

INTRODUCTION

Acts chapter 20 verses 28 – 31 says, "*Be on guard for yourselves and for all the flock, among which the Holy Spirit has made you overseers, to shepherd the church of God which He purchased with His own blood. I know that after my departure savage wolves will come in among you, not sparing the flock; and from among your own selves men will arise, speaking perverse things, to draw away the disciples after them. Therefore be on the alert, remembering that night and day for a period of three years I did not cease to admonish each one with tears.*"

Paul begins with a warning not only to the leadership but the sheep as well when he says, "take heed to yourselves and to the flock." Next of all, Paul assures these elders that they are there by Divine appointment when he says, "among which the Holy Spirit has made you overseers." According to this verse of scripture, there is no room for argument as to who places overseers in the church. Paul defines the reason for the warning when he says that wolves are coming. And when they come, they are not going to spare anyone, shepherds or sheep!

Paul defined the wolves as grievous, that is as vicious predators. I found it interesting that this aging apostle closed out his thoughts on this subject with this emotional statement, "Remember, I have warned you day and night for three years with tears in my eyes. The wolves are coming." There is no reason not to be ready.

However, before we begin this study on wolves I must give a strong word of caution. Leaders must be sure of their target before they fire! What if the suspected person turns out *not* to be a wolf, but rather a disobedient, angry sheep? Is it really a wolf or just a cranky sheep? It is certainly better for leaders to be cautious than to be caught unaware. Nevertheless, leaders should remember that when dealing with people, those people could easily be wounded for life.

It is true, angry sheep can appear wolf-like. And make no mistake about it, angry sheep can bite! So, leaders should take care. *"But if you bite and devour one another, take care that you are not consumed by one another."* (Galatians 5:15) Sheep should be handled differently than wolves – no matter how aggressively the sheep may act.

The wise leader can discern a lot about an individual's nature (that is if he or she is a wolf or a sheep) by observing the response of that individual when confronted. When innocent sheep are confronted they tend to become humble and submissive. When disobedient sheep are confronted they tend to bite. But when wolves are confronted they growl and become very aggressive.

CHAPTER ONE

The Wolves are Near

Before we delve into the dark world of the wolf and his ways, let's first take a look at the shepherd and the necessity for him to maintain his emotional footing. Sheep are never far from their shepherd. The old saying is, "As goes leadership, so goes the church." We see examples of this in the Old Testament. If the king served idols, the people eventually served idols. If the king served God, the nation eventually served God. Likewise, if the shepherd is in a deep depression, sooner or later, his sheep will come to the depressed place where he is. If the shepherd is angry and bitter he will raise an angry, bitter church.

Jim Jones is a sad example of a man that drew his sheep to the place where he was. Because he was an arrogant, self-absorbed, confused, and suicidal leader, he raised a people who were just as confused and eventually suicidal. What a tragedy, but what a truth.

Show me the place where the shepherd is dwelling, and I'll show you the place where his sheep (his church) will more than likely end up. If a pastor does not deal with his own issues, his issues will deal with him and eventually his church. Remember, sheep are never far from their shepherd; the church will reflect who he is.

Now, let me begin by identifying four basic kinds of people in every church:

1. Innocent sheep that must be protected
2. Disobedient sheep that must be corrected
3. Wolves in sheep's clothing (deception)
4. Undisguised wolves (nothing hidden)

Next, let me identify certain areas that wolves seek to control:

1. The church finances
2. The vision of the church
3. The doctrine being taught
4. The authority of the pastor
5. The direction of worship

The allure of success

Nothing attracts the attention of the wolf like success. It seems that the more you have, the more someone wants what you have. I use the example of someone who leaves his old, raggedy jacket on a bench in the mall. He can come back thirty minutes later and his raggedy jacket is still there. But if someone leaves a fine Corinthian leather jacket there, it will disappear in a heartbeat. In the same manner, no one wants the raggedy, in debt, struggling, small church. No one in their right mind is going to set out to steal something that is broken and failing. But let that church acquire property and finances, then everyone wants it, especially the wolf.

The successful, growing church provides many opportunities for the wolf. Which would be the more likely place for the wolf to hide, the church of twenty or the church of twenty thousand? The answer is obvious. It would be easier to go undetected in a church teaming with activity because of the sheer number of things going on at one time. Not only can one wolf hide there, but he can bring all of his friends with him as well. The larger the church, the more eyes are needed to watch it. Pastors must make sure that the eyes helping to watch are the eyes of those dedicated to the vision.

What about the small, struggling church? What opportunities does it provide for the wolf? The small, struggling church is easy to attack because it is more than likely run by one or two struggling people. This is the "sick" church, which to the wolf is like tracking a dying animal. Remember, the wolf is looking for opportunity. Successful or struggling, the wolf will stalk and attack when the conditions are in his favor.

Now let's look at certain points that the apostle Paul addresses in his departing statements to the Ephesian elders. One major point begins with these words: "after my departure." In essence Paul said, "I know *when I leave*, wolves *will* come." In other words, the presence of a strong shepherd keeps wolves at bay. Do not underestimate the importance of strong church leadership!

The second point Paul makes is, "Be on guard for yourselves and for all the flock, among which *the Holy Spirit has made you overseers*." Leaders are not hired, they are placed. This is the work of the Holy Spirit. The church did not just bring them in, but rather God sent them to that particular city. Hallelujah!

Jesus said, "I am the door of the sheep." (see John 10:7) Every sheepfold needs an established, strong gate. Jesus is the ultimate gate. Apostolic covering is the gate that strengthens and protects the local leadership. But the senior pastor* is the "strong gate" to the local church. Wolves will constantly ravage a church with weak or no leadership because there is no strong gate to protect the fold.

The wise pastor will also establish a strong eldership or leadership team around him, and it is crucial for this team to function as a unified group with a single vision or purpose. This unity at the top of the authority structure is essential in order to have unity throughout. Unity is like a precious oil flowing down. *"Behold, how good and how pleasant it is for brothers to dwell together in unity! It is like the precious oil upon the head, coming down upon the beard, even Aaron's beard, coming down upon the edge of his robes."* (Psalms 133:1-2) It flows from the head (the senior pastor) to the beard (the elders) on down to the robes (the people). Unity among leaders will result in a flow down to the sheep (the church), and elders are part of the "flow."

The next point that the apostle Paul makes that we want to look at is this: "savage wolves will come in among you." Notice that they come in. From where do they come? They come from outside the fence of the sheepfold. It is even likely that they come from another church. Make no mistake about it, wolves wander and wolves hunt. That is their nature.

The last and probably the most disturbing truth that Paul speaks is this: "and from among your own selves men will arise." Remember, this was written to the elders. This is referring to the wolf who rises up among the leadership. When I think of a wolf, I don't envision a pastor or an elder, but Paul clearly says, "from among your own selves men will arise."

What could cause an elder or a promising young minister to fall prey to a wolf-like nature? Perhaps he is overly ambitious. There is no shortage of personal ambition in the modern day church. He may crave success and fame. Worldly acclaim is like blood and meat to the leader who has not dealt with his own heart. Ministry is not about personal success. It is about God's Kingdom!

It is evident that Jesus has a Kingdom focus in the Lord's Prayer. *"... For thine is the kingdom, and the power, and the glory, forever."* (Matthew 6:13 KJV) The question here is clear. Whose kingdom are church leaders building? "For thine is the kingdom." What authority are church leaders walking in? "Thine is the power." Who is getting the praise and the credit? "Thine is the glory." Ultimately, the praise must go to God. While judging the motives of others, it is of utmost importance that leaders be open to have their own motives judged as well.

Knowing that wolves can and do arise from among the leadership, what evidence do we have that this has taken place? Again the apostle Paul tells us, "...speaking perverse things, to draw away disciples after them." There are two specific things that define this kind of wolf among the leadership. Number one, he is a false teacher; his method is "tickling the ear." He speaks a measure of truth seasoned with poison. Second, his motivation and purpose are to gather sheep to himself and away from the leadership team. He is self-serving. He manipulates people to follow him exclusively.

Perhaps this wolf is even someone raised up by the church leadership with high hopes of him or her becoming the next successor. No one can break a leader's heart like a spiritual son or daughter who has turned into a wolf. David said in Psalms 55: 12-13, *"For it is not an enemy who reproaches me, Then I could bear it; Nor is it one who hates me who has exalted himself against me, Then I could hide myself from him. But it is you, a man my equal, My companion and my familiar friend."* What a heartbreak!

With this in mind, I have a two-fold warning: Any preacher who does not point an individual to Christ is a wolf in sheep's clothing. Likewise, anyone who doesn't maintain the local shepherd's authority is a potential wolf among the sheep. He may be gathering the sheep to himself.

A number of years ago I was called on to speak for an entire week in a church that seemed to have everything in place. In those days we called those week long crusades "preaching a revival." I'm not sure what I revived, but I certainly kept a lot of dying programs on life support. I would sing and preach my heart out for barely enough money to feed my family. I ran out of gas more than once trying to get my antiquated motorhome to the next crusade. I did the best I knew how to do and God was certainly gracious not only to me, but to those who had to listen to me.

Anyway, back to our story. The pastor there was a happy and energetic leader, and the church was full. There were programs in place for every conceivable need. Everything was perfect, or so I thought. From the very first service I had an uneasy feeling regarding certain ones in leadership, and my concerns only grew stronger as the week continued. I had no proof of any dissension, and in fact all evidence pointed to the contrary. Still I could not shake the word of warning that God had placed in me. For six nights I spoke about the hidden agenda going on in the church that God was speaking to me about. Everything was okay for the first night or so, but then there grew a murmuring in the church concerning my unwillingness to change the direction of my messages. By the fifth night I think the church was ready to bring back public lynching, but I still couldn't shake the word of warning.

On the seventh night the pastor approached me and asked, "What are you going to speak on tonight?" I remember the look on his face when I said, "My message has not changed." In frustration he said to me, "My church is angry at you, but this isn't about you anymore. This church is ready to kick me out as well because of your word." Then he settled down a bit and said with a shaking voice, "Are you sure that you have heard a word from God?" To which I replied, "I'm sure."

I still remember the text I used on that final night. It was from the book of Hebrews chapter 13 verse 17 (KJV) *"Obey them that have the rule over you, and submit yourselves: for they watch for your souls, as they that must give account, that they may do it with joy, and not with grief: for that is unprofitable for you.*" Somewhere in the middle of this message I glanced over at the pastor who was sitting with his eyeglasses in his hand, staring straight forward. He was as pale as a man dying. I finished the message and walked away from the pulpit. There was no altar call given, I simply walked away.

The pastor still looked like death afterward, so I asked him if he was okay. He said to me, "I was so angry at you tonight that I could hardly stand to listen to you anymore." He then continued, "In that anger I said to God, 'If there is a hidden danger here in this church, show it to me.'" That pastor looked deep into my eyes and said, "If I ever heard a word from God, I heard it tonight." He said that the Spirit of the Lord spoke to him clearly and said, "Turn around, the enemy is behind you." When that pastor turned around, there directly behind him sat two of his leaders who had come in late.

As it turned out, those two leaders had been having secretive meetings with select people in the church. They were forming a plan to remove the pastor and take over. On the seventh night, the guilt was too great for some of those involved. They came forward and confessed their deception and intentions to the pastor. How devastating! He had personally handpicked those two leaders. In fact, one of the two was soon to be ordained and was to be at the pastor's right hand. But that wolf would not be content there; that wolf wanted the pastor's position.

The pastor struggled with the thought of, "Why didn't I see that?" I think there are two reasons he didn't see it. One is that the wolves were cautious as to whom they spoke. They were looking for people they thought would agree with them. The second reason is that the pastor had a trusting heart. He never dreamed that his own would turn against him. Although we don't want to walk in suspicion, it is imperative that we know them that labor among us. (see 1 Thessalonians 5:12) And that can only be accomplished through close personal relationship. Even in that, seemingly loving people can turn, and then the wolf tendencies come to the surface.

But whether the wolf comes in from outside the fence or is raised up within the leadership team, all wolves have the same result: "... not sparing the flock." They have either no love or false love for the sheep. They don't care whom they destroy. They are not there to help the leadership team to build the church. They deceive the sheep; they criticize and devour all for the purpose of achieving their personal goal.

CHAPTER TWO

The Wolf in the Pulpit

N ow that we know that a wolf can infiltrate the leadership of a local church, it is time to examine perhaps the most damaging position any wolf can have – the pulpit. Once again we turn to the Word of God.

> *"I wrote something to the church; but Diotrephes, who loves to be first among them, does not accept what we say. For this reason, if I come, I will call attention to his deeds which he does, unjustly accusing us with wicked words; and not satisfied with this, he himself does not receive the brethren, either, and he forbids those who desire to do so and puts them out of the church."*

This is an excerpt from a letter found in 3 John 1:9-10. This letter is not from just anyone. This is a letter from the apostle John, an apostle who was approved of by God Himself. But Diotrephes resisted John. In this short verse we can learn much about the character of Diotrephes, the wolf in the pulpit. I want us to look at four of Diotrephes' character traits.

First of all, we notice that the beloved apostle John says that Diotrephes loved "to be first among them." He had arrived at his position by his own power, which put him on very insecure and dangerous footing. His pride and arrogance were evident for he loved to be first. Clearly, he was ripe for a fall. *"Pride goes before destruction, And a haughty spirit before stumbling."* (Proverbs 16:18)

The problem with this kind of wolf is that when he falls, he usually takes his church down with him. Proud, arrogant preachers tend to build proud, arrogant churches. The saying I referred to earlier, "as goes leadership, so goes the church," is certainly true. It is essential that all leaders examine themselves and ask, "Where are we, as leaders, taking the church?" We do not want to set our church up for a fall.

The second problem we see in Diotrephes is that he spoke with malice towards authority. John wrote, "I will call attention to his deeds which he does, unjustly accusing us with wicked words." The wolf in the pulpit resists authority because godly authority can uncover him. He must convince the sheep that he is the ultimate authority and the only voice of truth. The wolf actually poisons the sheep by slandering those in authority over him, thereby isolating his flock from any outside connection. He is hiding his sheep.

The next character flaw we see in Diotrephes is closely connected to the previous one. He wanted no outside fellowship. John said that he did not receive the brethren; he was truly a lone wolf. He wanted no outside voices coming into his church. This trait reminds me of the scripture that says, "What fellowship has light with darkness?" (see 2 Corinthians 6:14) Perhaps he resisted godly fellowship because it would cast an immediate light on his dark character.

I personally dealt with one wolf who skillfully used the excuse of being too busy to fellowship. <u>This is a word from God:</u> If church leaders are too busy for godly fellowship, they are too busy! Let's face it, everyone will make time for the things they really want to do.

The last trait we need to look at is Diotrephes' method of pastoring his flock. His lack of love and insecurity were evident as he pastored with threats of punishment. John said, "He himself does not receive the brethren, either, and he forbids those who desire to do so and puts them out of the church." His philosophy was simple: "I am not submitted to anyone but myself. I make all the rules; I have no overseer. I want no counsel, and if you don't like it, there's the door!"

Personally, I am not too thrilled with preachers who use the expression, "It's my way or the highway." I have had to back up and retrace my steps too many times to believe that I have it all figured out. I know from my own personal experience that I need someone godly in my life to help me stay on course. Everyone should have a father in Christ. Every Timothy needs a Paul; every Elisha needs an Elijah. The apostle Paul said, "Follow me as I follow Christ." (see 1 Corinthians 11:1) Great men never become great all by themselves. Everyone needs a father in Christ.

"You younger men, likewise, be subject to your elders; and all of you, clothe yourselves with humility toward one another, for God is opposed to the proud, but gives grace to the humble. Therefore humble yourselves under the mighty hand of God, that He may exalt you at the proper time." (1 Peter 5:5-6) What a stark contrast God's method is to that of Diotrephes!

Peter said, "Submit, walk in humility, be humble, and *at the proper time...*" I repeat, the *proper time.* The term "proper time" in the Greek is "kairos." That means the right, proper, set time; precisely the correct time or season. In short, that means that it may not happen today, it may not happen tomorrow, but if a person is faithful, it will happen. And it will happen at just the right time.

CHAPTER THREE

The Wolf's Hunting Strategy

Now let me begin this chapter by pointing out to you the wolf's hunting strategy. In the natural, wolves hunt by separating the flock. They use the old "divide and conquer" tactic. I want to focus on the three areas that I see the spiritual wolf use in separating sheep in the church.

The first thing the wolf will try to do is to separate the weak Christians (sheep) from the strong ones. It is difficult to deceive that weak one who is surrounded by strong Christian fellowship. Therefore, the wolf must separate the weak from the strong. The wolf may look for that depressed "sheep" standing all by itself. That is a very vulnerable position for the sheep to be in. It is in the best interest of someone having an emotional struggle to go to local leadership for counsel and to surround him/herself with strong Christian fellowship.

Secondly, the wolf will try to separate the sheep from the shepherd's voice. In John chapter ten Jesus tells us that His sheep know His voice, and they will not follow another voice.

"Truly, truly, I say to you, he who does not enter by the door into the fold of the sheep, but climbs up some

other way, he is a thief and a robber. But he who enters by the door is a shepherd of the sheep. To him the doorkeeper opens, and the sheep hear his voice, and he calls his own sheep by name and leads them out. When he puts forth all his own, he goes ahead of them, and **the sheep follow him because they know his voice.** *A stranger they simply will not follow, but will flee from him, because* **they do not know the voice of strangers.**" (John 10:1-5 emphasis added)

A few years ago I had a fascinating conversation with a pastor on the subject of shepherds. (He has since gone on to be with the Lord and will be missed.) He told me of a true life example concerning sheep and the shepherd's voice. While on a bus tour in Israel, they came on a valley with literally hundreds of sheep grazing there. He asked the bus driver if they could stop long enough to take some pictures. It was there beside the road that he had a conversation with one of the many shepherds who were standing together. Because all of the sheep in the valley were from several different flocks, the pastor's question was obvious. "How do you know which of the sheep are yours?" To which the shepherd replied, "My sheep know me." While the pastor was still there taking pictures, one of the shepherds made a series of noises. One by one his sheep began to come out from this massive herd. In amazement the pastor watched as the shepherd's flock gathered to his side and followed him down the road. I remember the look on the pastor's face as he told the story, for he had actually witnessed this Bible principle first-hand. Those sheep knew their shepherd's voice. All he had to do was call them.

This principle is also true spiritually. So, if the wolf is going to establish his voice, he must first silence the voice of the local leadership. There are several ways the wolf can silence the shepherd's voice, but one of his most successful ways to accomplish this is through gossip. The wolf will sow seeds of suspicion among the sheep concerning the shepherd. He might cause the sheep to doubt the shepherd's integrity. The wolf knows that it is hard for a leader to regain the trust of the people once it is lost, even if the accusations that were made were untrue. Let's face it, people need little help when it comes to being suspicious. So, the wolf looks for opportunities to start rumors knowing that the people will take it from there.

This is a warning to the sheep (people): Everybody must be careful about things said concerning their shepherd, lest they *assist the wolf* in sowing discord and help the wolf in silencing their shepherd's voice. When we gossip, we are doing the work of the wolf.

> *"There are six things which the LORD hates, Yes, seven which are an abomination to Him: Haughty eyes, a lying tongue, And hands that shed innocent blood, A heart that devises wicked plans, Feet that run rapidly to evil,* **A false witness who utters lies, And one who spreads strife among brothers."**
> (Proverbs 6:16-19 emphasis added)

I have seen great men destroyed by gossip and slander. Let's all guard against becoming an ally of the wolf and destroying more men of God.

There is one last area of separation in which the wolf finds opportunity, and this is one he does not even need to work at. The shepherds do it to themselves; they separate from one another. The isolation of a shepherd is a sure way for him to become prey for the wolf. It never ceases to amaze me that there is such a lack of fellowship among pastors. We, as leaders, tend to criticize and talk about each other as if we were not on the same side. This kind of attitude is tailor made for the wolf to operate in. He focuses our attention on our differences rather than on the work at hand.

Just as I have warned the sheep, I now warn pastors and leaders: Be careful what you say about each other lest you, like the angry sheep, assist the wolf in silencing a fellow pastor's voice. Jesus said, *"By this all men will know that you are My disciples, **if you have love for one another.**"* (John 13: 35 emphasis added) Leaders should not allow differences to divide them from each other. They need to work it out!

Another reason fellowship among leaders (shepherds) is so important is because the diet of a shepherd is different from that of a sheep. Sheep eat grass and shepherds eat meat. Sheep can get healthy and fat eating grass, but a shepherd would starve on that diet. A shepherd can eat a steak, but sheep will turn up their noses at meat and walk on by looking for grass. Sheep cannot digest steak.

I have met very few sheep who really know what their shepherd needs. I love the sheep, but when I need fellowship and food for strength, I sit down with another shepherd. He or she will understand what I'm facing.

CHAPTER FOUR

The Wolf Pack

In nature wolves will hunt in packs. This also translates to a similar tactic in the church. When two or more wolves are working together in a local church, they may very well go directly after the senior pastor knowing that if they can smite the shepherd, they can scatter the sheep. (see Matthew 26:31 and Mark 14:27) It is easier for the wolf to single out the weak and vulnerable when the sheep are scattered and there is no leadership in place for their protection.

When the wolves are united in purpose it becomes essential that the shepherds also become united. The wolves will find it more difficult to defeat five shepherds than the one who stands alone. Ecclesiastes 4:12 says, *"And if one can overpower him who is alone, **two** can resist him. A cord of **three** strands is not quickly torn apart."* (emphasis added) The concept here is obvious; the more leaders stand together, the stronger they are.

Just as the leadership team in the local church must be united, so should leaders in the city or region be united. I strongly encourage pastors to run to the aid of a fellow pastor whom they see being ravaged by wolves. Leaders might sacrifice one of their services, perhaps a Sunday night, taking their people with them in order to attend that other pastor's service and show their support. Let the wolf see that this shepherd is not standing alone. An additional benefit to standing with a fellow pastor is that when the wolf leaves that church, chances are he won't come to the church belonging to the supporting pastor because the wolf knows that he has already been detected and uncovered.

I do, however, have a couple of cautions for leaders when they do this. One thing each pastor must guard against is a carnal tendency to see another church's destruction as an opportunity to gather more sheep for himself. But if he should unethically do so, he ought to be careful because he may be gathering in a disguised wolf as well as wounded sheep.

It is also important that the pastor under attack be assured that the fellow leaders are not there trying to gather his wounded sheep or to survey his pasture. They are only there for one purpose: To let the wolf know that, as leaders, we all stand united against him.

What I have been talking about here is leaders watching over each other and doing so with pure intentions. In a later chapter entitled "Forming a Network of Watchmen" I will discuss the concept of leaders becoming watchmen, not only over each other, but the city as well.

CHAPTER FIVE

Weak Fences

There is an old saying: "Strong fences make good neighbors." How true! While taking a tour of Disney's Animal Kingdom we saw what appeared to be lions and tigers running loose with gazelles and zebras. I remember wondering, "How do they keep the lions from eating the zebras?" We later learned that there were fences between the animals, but they were hidden from our sight. The fences protected the prey from the predators. They became "good neighbors." Likewise, strong walls or fences are needed to protect God's flock from vicious predators. These boundaries clearly differentiate between the place of God's will and protection, and the enemy's territory.

At the Animal Kingdom some fences were traditional fences, and others were electronic. Likewise, we have various boundaries or "fences" for the church (the sheep). Most of these "traditional fence" boundaries are set out for us in the Word of God. The rest are "electronic," so to speak. These fences are left up to the local leadership to place as they hear from God and find His will or vision for their local church.

When God says, "Don't do it," that is a fence line, and the message is clear. Sometimes, though, we are tempted to bend His directives a bit. As an illustration, if someone is on a lonely country road and the sign at the crossroads says, "STOP," is that person obligated to stop if no one else is at the intersection? Yes! The sign does not say, "Stop at your own discretion." It says, "STOP," and the driver must stop. If an individual gets in the habit of running stop signs, he may some day run one at an intersection that is filled with traffic.

I saw a tragic story on a reality program about a senseless traffic death. A man lost his life when he ran a stop sign, and his vehicle was hit broadside. The authorities said, "He died instantly." What a horrific end to a man's life. But what makes this story even more tragic is that he had been ticketed numerous times for running that very same stop sign. He had been warned time after time, but for whatever reason, he made the decision to run that stop sign one last time. He paid a high price for his failure to stay within legal "boundaries."

Our tendency in the church to bend God's directives also breaks down our boundaries or fences, if you will. When the word says, "Don't gossip", it means don't gossip. When we gossip, we bend and weaken the fence. When leadership says, "This is the policy of this church," that is a boundary or a fence. When people argue with the policy, they bend and weaken the fence. When the fence breaks down it provides easy access for the wolf to come in and ravage the flock.

So the reality is that not only will the church have wolves circling the fence trying to get in, but at times there will be angry sheep pushing on the fence trying to get out. Those disgruntled sheep can weaken that fence by pushing on it. They want out not realizing that there is no protection outside the fence.

So the sheep push the boundaries, or if you will, they lean on the fence. They argue with the pastor's decision; they gossip over dinner. By doing so, they weaken the fence, and incidentally, they poison their own family at the same time.

The wolf looks for the place where the sheep themselves have been pushing on the fence, therefore weakening the church's defenses. The longer the rebellious sheep gather there, the more other innocent sheep will join them wondering what all the fuss is about. What began as a small issue has now caught the attention of the wolf. The concept is simple: The rebellious sheep want out and the wolf wants in. Without realizing it, the disobedient sheep have created the perfect entrance for the wolf.

People who are constantly criticizing the pastor, the elders, and the church are endangering the entire flock. For the sake of the innocent sheep the leaders must take action. They must take the rebellious sheep to the gate and turn them loose. If those disgruntled sheep break out through the fence, the wolf will have free access to the entire flock. It is better for the church to lose a few than to lose many.

Sometimes leaders are reluctant to do this. Perhaps it is a matter of pride for the shepherd. Leaders do not want to appear as if they are unable to keep all who come to them. But not all who come to them are there to join with them. Even Jesus Himself had Judas Iscariot. (see John 17:12)

And of course, every community has what I call the "floating Christian." They "float" from church to church with a critical heart. No church is quite good enough for them. If left unchecked in the church, their critical spirit will infect the other sheep. The floating, critical Christian in any church is one of the wolf's best allies inside the fence. Leaders cannot let them stay. The leaders must take them to the gate and turn them loose.

CHAPTER SIX

The Wolf is Circling the Fence

I had a pastor come to me in a panic and say, "Man, you've got to pray for me." When I asked him what the problem was he told me of a pattern that all of us have experienced in life. He said, "Every two years or so, I face the same personal battle. It's like clockwork." His battleground happened to be depression. He continued, "I'll face it, win the battle, and think, well that's that!" Then about two years later he would face it again. Leaders are saying the same thing. "My church will face a certain problem and win. Then so many years later, we face the same thing all over again."

We can all relate, but do we know what is happening? I do! Look at the pattern. The attack comes, the individual or church wins, the problem goes away, then two years later (or whatever the time frame is) it's back. The answer is simple. The wolf is circling the fence! Form this picture in your mind: Visualize a wolf sniffing along the bottom of the fence looking for a place to get in. He stops here and there along the way just long enough to dig a little. He is looking for a place where the boundaries will yield. Constantly on the move, he will test every square foot of the perimeters looking for a place to get in. The wolf circles the fence day after day, year after year. If he doesn't find anything over there, then he will come back and dig at the same damaged place where he almost got in before. He will continue his relentless walk around the life of the individual or the church, until he has either been successful in breaching the fence or he has been destroyed.

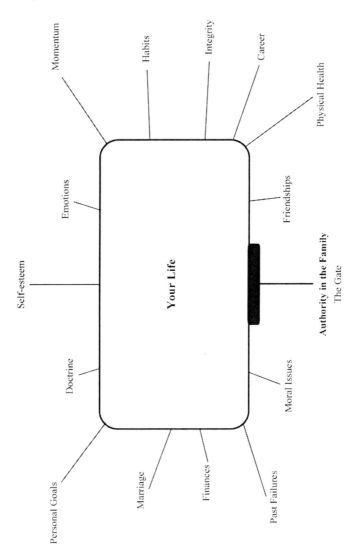

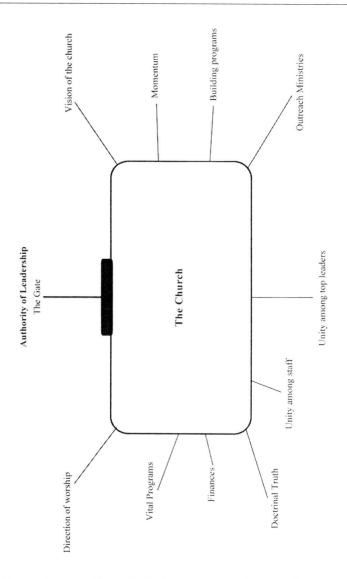

Strengthen the fence! Work on overcoming weaknesses
and seek counseling.
Maintain the fence! Use the Word and prayer
to develop relationship with God.
Defend the fence! Determination – Make a stand.

CHAPTER SEVEN

The Wolf in Sheep's Clothing

We have all heard the expression "wolf in sheep's clothing." Wow, this is going to be a tough one to cover because we are looking for our enemy *inside* the fence. This wolf has already very successfully infiltrated the church. It's easy to spot the wolf outside the fence, because he's the only one out there. Shepherds and sheep are inside; the wolf is outside. But when dealing with the wolf hiding among the sheep we find this predator is prowling on the inside among us. He is so well disguised that if you throw him out there in the middle of a hundred other sheep, you can't see him. He is there every Sunday, he never misses a work day, but the people have no idea that he, a wolf, is there. This is a very real threat because this wolf is in plain sight, but no sees him.

One evening as I was cruising through the television channels in search of something worthwhile to watch, I came across a fascinating special on the American Indian culture. Because they hunted with bow and arrow which had a limited range and limited accuracy, it was necessary for them to devise a plan to get closer to their prey. So these resourceful hunters would put on the skin of an animal, crawl like an animal, and make sounds like an animal, all for the purpose of closing the distance between the hunter and the hunted. They appeared to be of no threat. They had mastered the art of deception.

In today's culture, we are not that skilled. We throw corn on the ground, sit in a tree, and wait for some unsuspecting critter to come and eat. Then we cut loose with a high powered rifle at close range and ... Well, you have probably come to the conclusion by now that I am not a hunter. But the point I am trying to make here is this: If you want to get close to your prey, disguise your intentions.

Do you want to know what's frightening to me? This wolf has blended in so perfectly that not only do the sheep not see him, but often the pastor hasn't spotted him, either. Pastors need not feel bad if they have been deceived by a wolf, because he really has developed the perfect disguise. He or she at times can be very charming which only adds to the illusion of being no danger.

This clever wolf will often position himself next to the deceived pastor, which gives him or her credibility with the sheep. He may publicly praise the pastor while secretly undermining his authority. This is truly a wolf hidden among the sheep.

Once the wolf has cleverly disguised himself in the clothing of a sheep he has a wide range of tactics and avenues that he may take advantage of to accomplish his own agenda. It will serve us well to take a closer look at some of these particular skills and tactics he may employ.

Let's begin by realizing that this wolf is a skillful actor. In fact, he can many times mimic godly leadership. He may watch and study the man of God in order to perfect his imitation by learning the shepherd's ways. He knows how to deceive, and he knows the right things to say. He can fill a pulpit or teach a class.

He may mimic the nature of the sympathetic leader. He finds out what is troubling the sheep and then sympathizes with their cause. He convinces the sheep with soothing words that he shares their concern. The wolf knows that sheep with a cause are very easy to get next to. And unfortunately, it is not hard to deceive people. In reality, he may or may not care about the sheep's concerns. He may simply see an opportunity to promote his own agenda.

The wolf knows that most sheep cannot tell the difference between true anointing and sparkling personality. My good friend, Pastor Louis Bartet, calls this bigger than life wolf "The Amazing Steve Stunning." (I sincerely apologize if there is, in fact, a godly minister somewhere out there named Steve Stunning.) While we do not want to brand everyone with a great personality as being a wolf, the wolf certainly does know how to use his personality. He uses it to counterfeit the anointing and sway the people. In the church's eagerness to see the miraculous, character is often ignored in search of signs and wonders. It is up to righteous leaders to protect the often gullible sheep from these wolves in disguise.

Wolves have mastered the art of transformation, and scripture gives clear warning of this:

> *"For such men are false apostles, deceitful workers, disguising themselves as apostles of Christ. No wonder, for even Satan disguises himself as an angel of light. Therefore it is not surprising if his servants also disguise themselves as servants of righteousness, whose end will be according to their deeds."* (2 Corinthians 11:13-15)

Leaders need to be able to detect this kind of wolf.

CHAPTER EIGHT

Wolf Footprints and the Shepherd's Reputation

So, how can a leader detect a wolf in sheep's clothing? By checking his footprints! Wolves leave a distinctive footprint of destruction behind them. Just follow his footprints backwards, and ask the questions: "Where has he been?" "Who has he been running with?" This wolf can be followed from church to church to see the destruction he has left behind. His footprints always have traces of innocent blood on them. Just follow the blood trail back to the shepherds and sheep he has slain.

A lot can be told about a person by looking at his "running buddies." I'm not sure who said it, but it's a great saying: "Show me your friends and I'll show you your future." That wolf hasn't always been in sheep's clothing. He has been in the company of other wolves.

Once a wolf in sheep's clothing has been identified, how does the leader target this enemy? This is a very difficult situation to deal with because when action is taken against this wolf, to the other innocent sheep who are watching it appears that leadership is abusing another innocent sheep. The sheep don't see the vicious wolf; they only see the wool.

Remember, he is in the perfect disguise. If the wolf is a person who is well liked in the church, it can be double trouble.

How can leaders deal with an enemy that the people don't see as the enemy? To begin with, pastors or leaders must be aware that as they start to deal with this wolf, the sheep may very well brand that leader as an intolerant or abusive shepherd. Remember that the sheep probably have not yet spotted the wolf. In their eyes, it appears that leadership is becoming abusive. This is the time when leadership will hear such statements as, "How could he do that to dear old Sister Smith?" or "Brother Jones has been a respected member of this church for years."

Every pastor will at some point or another have to pass the "who's in authority" test. For one young, idealistic, novice pastor his test came in the first year of his first church. There was in that church an old retired preacher. He was a powerful self-proclaimed champion of the sheep who would not submit to the younger leader's authority. When confronted, the wolf growled, "I was here before you came, and I will be here when you're gone!" That old wolf had controlled that church and was responsible for the loss of at least three or four pastors. But, the new shepherd stood his ground against the wolf and won. I am not saying that he didn't take some criticism, because he did. He took a verbal beating from the entire community before the truth finally came out. The wolf eventually died, but not before he did everything in his power to destroy that young pastor. Even the pastor's denomination questioned his motives for a time, but he survived. Today, thirty years later, that pastor is still leading the church and has established his name in the city.

I know criticism hurts, but may I remind everyone that a leader's job is not to protect himself from hurt, but rather to protect God's sheep from the wolf. Leaders must do their job and leave their reputation to God.

*"I am the good shepherd; **the good shepherd lays down His life for the sheep.** He who is a hired hand, and not a shepherd, who is not the owner of the sheep, sees the wolf coming, and leaves the sheep and flees, and the wolf snatches them and scatters them. **He flees because he is a hired hand** and is not concerned about the sheep. I am the good shepherd, and I know My own and My own know Me, even as the Father knows Me and I know the Father; and I lay down My life for the sheep. I have other sheep, which are not of this fold; I must bring them also, and they will hear My voice; and they will become one flock with one shepherd."* (John 10:11-16 emphasis added)

A hireling will not lay down his life for the sheep because other things (i.e. comfort, position, status, financial security, or reputation) are more important to him. A true shepherd will pick up his rod and staff and protect his sheep, but the hireling will run from the wolf at the first sign of trouble. David said in Psalms 23:4 *"Yea, though I walk through the valley of the shadow of death I will fear no evil for thou art with me; **thy rod and thy staff** they comfort me."* (KJV emphasis added)

We will cover the details for actually taking down this wolf in sheep's clothing later in the chapter on "Scripturally Uncovering the Wolf."

CHAPTER NINE

The Wolf that Prophesies (False Prophets)

Matthew 7:15 says, *"Beware of the **false prophets**, who come to you in sheep's clothing, but inwardly are **ravenous wolves**."* This is a direct warning that we must not ignore.

There are many sad tales of destruction left by this type of wolf, and one perfect example of this comes from a dear friend of mine who operates in the genuine prophetic gift. There were two churches involved, one of which was small, but successful, with strong leadership. The other was in the process of being torn apart due to a pastor with obvious emotional problems. In the successful church there was a man who claimed to be a prophet and had tried on a number of occasions to convince the pastor to elevate him. He was repeatedly denied because of his unethical practices. His tactic was to prophesy without leadership's approval and to draw the weak to himself in an effort to form his own following. Because of a strong, godly pastor the false prophet was rebuked and forced to sit down.

A disgruntled couple had left the struggling church and come to the successful one where they met the false prophet.

He immediately befriended them and an alliance was formed. When the frustrated couple relayed the story of the despair in the church they had left, the false prophet saw this as an opportunity to find a new home with new opportunities to promote himself. Because there was some distance between the two churches and two different denominations involved, no alarm had been sent to the next pastor.

For one full year the wolf remained hidden and quiet. But soon after the year was over, the wolf began his hunt. He went from praying around the altars with others present to singling out sheep to pray with them in private. Then he began to prophesy to the weak and to convince them that he was the new prophetic voice in the church. His next tactic was to start home meetings, but not in his own home because that would have been a red flag to someone. So he convinced a gullible young leader in the church to begin the meetings in his home, but the wolf would be the voice.

Because the pastor was weak and insecure, he never recognized the wolf. He only saw this as gaining a fresh, new elder, and he thought he could align himself with a voice the people seemed to embrace. Soon after the wolf began to gain control, my friend, an elder's wife, spoke up and said, "Something is not right here." Her warning went to her husband who also had grown suspicious of this man's ways. Unfortunately, when warned, the weak, insecure pastor took the wolf's side.

The wolf then saw his opportunity to strengthen his own position and destroy those who could uncover him. He "prophesied" against anyone who stood in his way. He discredited godly elders and set himself up as the pastor's "in-house prophet."

His downfall came when the couples who were closest to him began to have serious family problems. He had observed these people long enough to have first hand knowledge of their lives and would then publicly prophesy over them as if he heard it from God. The deception was over! The disillusioned and wounded church, all but destroyed, never recovered. After some investigation it was learned that this false prophet had destroyed at least three churches.

Scripture says I Corinthians 14:29 (KJV) *"Let the prophets speak two or three, and* **let the others judge**." (emphasis added) If a prophet is convinced that he or she has heard a word from God, he or she will willingly submit the word to be judged. A true prophet not only walks in authority, but is also submitted to true apostolic authority.

CHAPTER TEN

The Wolf on the Official Board

This wolf willingly offers to become the voice of the people, assuring them that if they will vote him in on the board that he will carry their cause. Once he is hidden on the church board he can make the most of this golden opportunity to use his newly found authority to reproach the pastor. He is now also in a position to cast his vote and apply more pressure against leadership. He will more than likely use the sheep's complaints to accuse the shepherd. He will listen to everything the sheep say, looking for an opportunity to accuse leadership. But remember, it is Satan who is the accuser of the brethren. (see Revelation 12:10)

The wolf on the board cleverly positions himself behind the wishes and desires of the people. He rarely says, "Pastor, I have an issue with you." It is usually, "The people have an issue with you." He has hidden himself within the sheep's complaints. When a wolf says that everyone is unhappy, it usually means that there are two or three angry sheep with a complaint against the leader. The wolf on the church board may use this statement to formulate an attack against the leadership using apparent concern for the people's well-being. He may see this as his chance to begin gathering the sheep to himself. Many times he will embellish the number of critics to bring fear or dismay to the leader's heart.

Fortunately, leaders can take courage with this promise: *"For God hath not given us the spirit of fear; but of power, and of love, and of a sound mind."* (2 Timothy 1:7 KJV)

The wolf on the church board appears to be the protector of the sheep, but in reality, his agenda becomes self-serving:

1. Gain the confidence of the sheep.
2. Use the sheep's complaints to smite the shepherd.
3. Set himself up as the new visionary.
4. Take ownership of the flock.
5. Begin preaching a perverse gospel.

It is important for me to say at this point that not every complaint from the sheep is unfounded. The sheep need to be able to voice their concerns to the elders if there is something troubling them. If someone says to a leader, "This is what the people are saying," it must not be disregarded offhand. Elders need to make sure that there is no truth in the accusation or concern. If there is, corrective steps should be taken. I would rather be shown my error than walk another day damaging the sheep I was called to protect. True elders are in place not only to help guard the sheep, but to be counsel and godly support to the shepherd (senior pastor) as well.

When a complaint is voiced, leaders also must determine who is speaking, a wolf or a timid elder? Leaders must look at the character and motive of the man speaking. As I stated, the wolf on the board will use the "everyone is unhappy" statement to formulate an attack against the leadership using apparent concern for the people's well-being. The timid elder, however, uses the same statement, but his motive is different. He is afraid of offending someone. He is desperately trying to be on everyone's side. But let's look at the angel that Joshua confronted outside the city of Jericho. (see

Joshua 5) When Joshua asked him, *"Are you for us or for our adversaries?"* The angel answered, *"No, rather I come as captain of the host of the Lord!"* (see verses 13 & 14) In other words, "I am not on your side nor am I on their side. But as a representative of God, "I am here to carry out His will."

I, myself, have had to tell more than one church, "I am not on the pastor's side, or the elder's side, or the church's side. I am here to represent the will of God in this situation." We *cannot be on everyone's side*; we are there as a spokesman for God. Godly elders are called to carry out the will of God. This is not a "church's will" issue, this is a "God's will" issue.

CHAPTER ELEVEN

The Danger of Voting

B ut let's consider something about the time when "everyone is unhappy." When should leaders let the sheep have what they want? I guess the real issue is what does the leadership team want the people to have control over? Should the sheep have control over the vision of the church? NO! God always gives control of the vision to the pastor and his elders. Personally, I don't mind the ladies choosing the color of the carpet or the décor in the auditorium. I don't mind the men determining if we have a center isle or two on the sides. But when it comes to the vision and direction of the church, that is not up for a vote!

Leaders know their people. Probably not many of the people are truly spiritual enough to guide the church, or have the discernment to spot the wolf in sheep's clothing. That is part of the problem with church voting. Voting leads people to believe that they have *ownership* of the church rather than *stewardship* in the church. Sheep are not over the vision; they are part of the vision.

The problem with voting is very simple. I can explain by giving a hypothetical situation. Suppose God speaks to the leadership and say's, "Do this!" (whatever "this" is) So the church votes. When the votes are counted, there are so many for and so many against. It doesn't take a spiritual giant to determine that someone has missed God. Someone has actually voted against God's will.

But the question may be posed, "If 'this' affects the people, shouldn't they have a say?" That simply brings me back to the original thought: *God* said, "Do this." He didn't say, "Find out what the people think." He didn't say, "Talk the people into doing this." He just said, "Do this." At no point did God ask Moses to find out what the people thought or to talk the people into leaving Egypt. He simply told Moses to lead them. I think many times leaders spend too much time trying to talk the people into doing the will of God (especially when people have the vote), and not enough time leading them into it.

If sheep know what is best for themselves, why did God establish shepherds to watch over them? A wise man once said, "People always know what they want, but rarely know what they need. The problem with getting what they want is they must live with what they get."

There is a grave danger in giving the people everything that they want. Just look at Israel. Israel said, "Give us a king like all the other nations." (see 1 Samuel 8:5-7) God had established their government, but they wanted an earthly king like the other earthly nations. They said, "This is what we want. Give it to us!" God warned them in 1 Samuel 8: 11-19: *"He said, 'This will be the procedure of the king who will reign over you: he will take your sons and place them for himself in his chariots and among his horsemen and they will run before his chariots. He will appoint for himself commanders of thousands and of fifties, and some to do his plowing and to reap his harvest and to make his weapons of war and equipment for his chariots. He will also take your daughters for perfumers and cooks and bakers. He will take the best of your fields and your vineyards and your olive groves and give them to his servants. He will take a tenth of your seed and of your vineyards and give to his officers and to his servants. He will also take your male servants and your female servants and your best young men and your donkeys and use them for his work. He will take a tenth of your flocks, and you yourselves will become his servants.* ***Then you will cry out in that day because of your king whom you have chosen for yourselves, but the LORD will not answer you in that day.*** *' Nevertheless, the people refused to listen to the voice of Samuel, and they said, 'No, but there shall be a king over us.'"* (emphasis added) So God gave them the king they desired, and look at what happened. They had to live with what they got.

If leaders give the people everything they want there will be consequences. Much like fathers, pastors and leaders cannot always give in to the wishes of the people just because they want something. If my five year-old granddaughter wants to have my loaded handgun, it doesn't mean that I'm obligated to give it to her. The consequences would be too grave.

The wolf, on the other hand, is liable to give the people anything they desire to further his own agenda resulting in undermining, disruption, or otherwise putting the sheep in dangerous situations. His top priority is always achieving his goal, regardless of the consequence.

CHAPTER TWELVE

The Wolf and his Money

I n this chapter let's talk for a moment or two about the wolf and his money. This is a very serious matter, so let me begin by identifying four basic types of givers in the church.

1. The Cheerful Giver. This person gives with no personal agenda. *"Each one must do just as he has purposed in his heart, not grudgingly or under compulsion, for God loves a cheerful giver."* (2 Corinthians 9:7)
2. The Sacrificial Giver. This person, like the widow giving her coins, sacrifices when he or she gives. *"A poor widow came and put in two small copper coins, which amount to a cent. Calling His disciples to Him, He said to them, 'Truly I say to you, this poor widow put in more than all the contributors to the treasury; for they all put in out of their surplus, but she, out of her poverty, put in all she owned, all she had to live on.'"* (Mark 12:42-44)
3. The Pharisaical Giver. This person gives to be noticed, trying to gain reputation and acclaim. Jesus warned the disciples not to be like the Pharisees who

did things for the purpose of being noticed. (see Luke 20:47 and Matthew 6: 1-6)
4. The Wolf Giver. The wolf gives in order to gain favor and control. He may often use his money to "buy" a position rather than be placed by God.

There is no doubt about it, sheep have a tendency to vote the wealthy into ministry. They confuse wealth or financial savvy with spirituality. Financial success should never be confused with the approval of God upon a man's life. The world is full of successful men who do not serve God. A godly man who is also successful is a rare and wonderful gift.

Sadly, a man's wealth and willingness to give financially to a church may also cause leaders to overlook his character. When a person expresses interest in ministry and has financial means, it is so easy to ignore the red flags and view this as being the provision from God to the church. Leaders must always bear in mind that scriptural qualifications should never be overlooked when choosing a leadership team.

*"It is a trustworthy statement: if any man aspires to the office of **overseer**, it is a fine work he desires to do. An **overseer**, then, must be above reproach, the husband of one wife, temperate, prudent, respectable, hospitable, able to teach, not addicted to wine or pugnacious, but gentle, peaceable, free from the love of money. He must be one who manages his own household well, keeping his children under control with all dignity (but if a man does not know how to manage his own household, how will he take care of the church of God?), and not a new convert, so that he will not become conceited and fall into the condemnation incurred by the devil. And he must have a good reputation with those outside the church,*

so that he will not fall into reproach and the snare of the devil. **Deacons** *likewise must be men of dignity, not double-tongued, or addicted to much wine or fond of sordid gain, but holding to the mystery of the faith with a clear conscience. These men must also first be tested; then let them serve as deacons if they are beyond reproach.* **Women** *must likewise be dignified, not malicious gossips, but temperate, faithful in all things. Deacons must be husbands of only one wife, and good managers of their children and their own households. For those who have served well as deacons obtain for themselves a high standing and great confidence in the faith that is in Christ Jesus."* (1 Timothy 3:1-13 emphasis added)

Yes, money can be a real temptation especially to the struggling, small church. Don't get me wrong, the church needs finances to operate. The old saying goes, "We are not in it for the money, but without the money we are not in it." And that saying is true. But, money in the wrong hands can be very dangerous. I do not want the wolf's money!

Let's look at a story about money from scripture: *"Now there was a man named Simon, who formerly was practicing magic in the city and astonishing the people of Samaria, claiming to be someone great; ... Even* **Simon himself believed***; and after being baptized, he continued on with Philip, and as he observed signs and great miracles taking place, he was constantly amazed. ... Now when Simon saw that the Spirit was bestowed through the laying on of the apostles' hands,* **he offered them money, saying, 'Give this authority to me as well***, so that everyone on whom I lay my hands may receive the Holy Spirit.'* **But Peter** *said to him, 'May your silver perish with you, because you thought you could obtain the gift of God with money! You have no part or portion in this matter, for your heart is not right before*

God. Therefore repent of this wickedness of yours, and pray the Lord that, if possible, the intention of your heart may be forgiven you.'" (Acts 8:9, 13,18-22 emphasis added)

In this story the newly converted Simon tried to buy authority that was not his. He could have easily become a wolf. But Peter, being a wise apostle, confronted him, and Simon repented. Notice the value of the presence of a strong leader.

In like manner, pastors and leaders must be very discerning because there are wolves who will attempt to use their money to buy what is not rightfully theirs. I say again, leaders must never put anyone into ministry because he or she can financially help the church. People should be placed because they are called and anointed for the position. We are not building a business, we are building the Kingdom. The apostle Paul admonishes us in 1 Timothy chapter five that we should not be hasty in laying our hands on anyone. *"Do not lay hands upon anyone **too hastily** and thereby share responsibility for the sins of others; keep yourself free from sin."* (1 Timothy 5:22 emphasis added) We should know them. The leader must know the values and know the character of the individual before proceeding.

As a practical illustration of the points that I am making, I would like to give you a couple of experiences from real life that I have had involving two different churches. In the first church the wolf, in effect, bought the pastor and guided the church with bribes and gifts. This shepherd was so needy that he mistook this for God's provision. Yes, the pastor had a new car, but the church had "strange fire" burning within. (see Numbers 26:61)

I know full well that financial gain is a difficult lure for a leader to ignore, particularly when finances are a disaster. Perhaps that leader had small children, and they were looking to their father for toys at Christmas. I myself have been there, staring into the eyes of my children who were asking for a dollar for a candy bar that I could not afford. It was very painful, and I hurt. But by the grace of God my children and I survived and, in fact, were blessed by learning to trust God in the hard times.

> *"Then He said to them, 'Beware, and be on your guard against every form of greed; for not even when one has an abundance does his life consist of his possessions.'"* (Luke 12:15)

Leaders must beware for the wolf will look for the needy (and perhaps) covetous shepherd. Ministry is not about the abundance of things a leader possesses, but rather about *who* that leader is. It is of the utmost importance that leaders value their relationship with God and His anointing on their lives above all else.

When the pastor and the elders refuse the wolf's lure, he will probably withhold his finances altogether to apply pressure on the leaders. But the leadership team can fortify themselves with the knowledge that God is their source. Philippians 4:19 can be their weapon against the lure of the wolf and the pressure he tries to apply. *"And my God will supply all your needs according to His riches in glory in Christ Jesus."* The Philippians gave to God's purposes. The great apostle Paul certainly was confident that God would meet the needs of people with Kingdom priorities.

This is the account of the second church I want to bring to your attention. A young pastor and his family took the pastorate of a small, struggling church. There were two brothers in the church who had always controlled the church with their wealth. They were wolves! They did not like the fact that this new, young pastor was beginning to take the church in a fresh, new direction. Because the church was greatly in debt, the district office of their denomination was eager to rid themselves of the debt-ridden property and its on-going problems. These two brothers offered to buy the building from the denomination and pay off its debts. This obviously looked like they were trying to help. The denomination agreed to sell, and the trap was set. The two brothers immediately fired the pastor and put his family out on the street. Then, much to my surprise, the denomination re-issued a charter to those two men allowing them to reopen under a new church name. The two brothers continued to control and rule the church with no shepherd in place to stop them. In no uncertain terms, they bought control of the church.

Money being used to influence is as old as money itself. Judas and thirty pieces of silver are synonymous with the selling of our Savior. *"Then one of the twelve, named Judas Iscariot, went to the chief priests and said, 'What are you willing to give me to betray Him to you?' And they weighed out **thirty pieces of silver** to him. From then on he began looking for a good opportunity to betray Jesus."* (Matthew 26:14-16 emphasis added)

CHAPTER THIRTEEN

Wolf-like Logic – The Ends Justifies the Means

The wolf can cause a great deal of confusion by taking a beautiful Bible truth and taking it out of balance. I think all of us have had a change of heart at one time or another as to what we believe and why. We have had to bring our doctrine back into balance from time to time. The wolf isn't interested in balance; he is interested in his own goals.

Let's focus on one of the beautiful promises that God gives us, namely financial blessing and provision. But as with so many things that God say's, there is always someone out there looking for a way to use that truth to his or her advantage. The wolf views the tender, giving heart of the Christian as his opportunity to divert money from legitimate Kingdom work.

Remember, the wolf works primarily through deception. Have you ever heard anyone say, "Yes, we were a little deceptive, but we raised the money for a good cause?" In other words does it really matter how we get there as long as we get there? Does the ends justify the means? What takes place when we abuse truth, and what's more, do it in front of the world?

Does God want us to prosper? You bet! Does God bless the cheerful, willing giver? Absolutely. The problem comes when someone takes God's truths and bends them a little in order to serve his own purpose. It is so important to keep scripture in focus and balance, because the world is watching.

A good friend of mine who is a pre-believer was sitting in his living room watching a local minister raise money for his cause. I was surprised to see my friend, "LJ," watching a Christian program, so I joined him. Somewhere along the way, the preacher said, "If you don't help me with your finances, I am off the air." At that moment I could see where the inevitable train wreck was about to take place, and I couldn't do a thing about it. Here is my pre-believer friend watching a preacher in need, and I remember thinking, "This is not going to have a happy ending." The preacher made a statement that I have heard so many times before. He said, "If you will send me 'x-amount' of dollars, God will return it to you ten-fold." My heart started to skip beats because I knew "LJ" was going to voice his opinion on this one. "LJ" looked at me with a smile and said, "If that's true, and God is going to return it ten-fold, then why doesn't he send me 'x-amount' of dollars and let God give him a ten-fold return?" "LJ" continued, "Wouldn't it make him more money, a ten-fold return on his investment?" I had no answer. Is it any wonder that the world doesn't trust us?

The preacher continued, "If you love God, you will sit down right now, write out that check, and send it to me." Wait a minute, "If you love God, you will support me?" Wow! What a dangerous statement to send out over the air waves. More than that, what a marketing ploy! How in the world did he tie my love for God into the support of his ministry? He is not my pastor. I don't attend his church. But he just told me that if I don't support him with my finances, I can't possibly love God. Listen one more time to what he said: "If you love God, sit down and write a check to me."

Now I am not in any way saying that this man was a wolf. I know that times are tough, and many have hit the airwaves looking for financial support. But while the Christian may have understood the minister's concept of a ten-fold blessing, may I remind leaders that the world is watching – listening as well, and they don't get it! We must remember that's why they call it "public broadcasting." What "LJ" needed was the gospel of Jesus Christ. What he got was a lesson in unethical Christian economics.

I witnessed another preacher taking his own offering, and he said, "God told me that there is *an individual* (one person) here who is going to give a check for $1,000.00. Three people responded. Did he give back the other two checks? No, he kept it all. I wonder how much is said in the excitement of the moment, but then followed by the all confirming statement, "God said."

In Ezekiel 22:25-28 it says, *"There is a conspiracy of her prophets in her midst like a roaring lion tearing the prey. They have devoured lives; they have taken treasure and precious things; they have made many widows in the midst of her. Her priests have done violence to My law and have profaned My holy things; they have made no distinction between the holy and the profane, and they have not taught the difference between the unclean and the clean; and they hide their eyes from My sabbaths, and I am profaned among them. Her princes within her are **like wolves tearing the prey**, by shedding blood and destroying lives in order to get dishonest gain. Her prophets have smeared whitewash for them, seeing false visions and divining lies for them, saying, 'Thus says the Lord GOD,' **when the LORD has not spoken.**"* (emphasis added)

How important is it for leaders to be ethical in their financial dealings and fund raising? Remember, the world is watching us.

In order to bring accountability and be a covering for each other, a pastor friend and I had a question that we would ask each other moments before we would enter the pulpit to bring the word of God. We would simply say, "Are you preaching truth or working an angle?" It would serve each of us leaders to ask ourselves that same question before we speak. Am I working an angle on God's people?

If there is any other doctrine that the wolf in the pulpit has taken more advantage of than that of prosperity, I don't know what it would be. The greedy leader takes biblical principles, like financial blessings and prosperity, then he preaches them for his own personal gain. The unscrupulous wolf fleeces the sheep then lines his den with their wool. All this is done under the disguise of funding God's work.

Not everyone who raises funds for the cause of Christ is a wolf. But I can guarantee you, in among the righteous fund raisers lurk the wolves in preacher's clothing. They see the ministry as a great personal financial treasure chest. The leadership team must be on their guard against this very thing.

Luke 12:15 says, *"Then He said to them, 'Beware, and be on your guard against every form of greed; for not even when one has an abundance does his life consist of his possessions.'"*

Just as unethical as the leader who takes the sheep's money for his personal gain, is the one who shows *preferential treatment* in order to get financial support. Leader's must love and protect all of the sheep under their care. A leader showing preferential treatment to someone because they can bless the church financially, is at best ungodly and scripturally unethical.

"My brethren, do not hold your faith in our glorious Lord Jesus Christ with an attitude of personal favoritism. For if a man comes into your assembly with a gold ring and dressed in fine clothes, and there also comes in a poor man in dirty clothes, and you pay special attention to the one who is wearing the fine clothes, and say, 'You sit here in a good place,' and you say to the poor man, 'You stand over there, or sit down by my footstool,' have you not made distinctions among yourselves, and become judges with evil motives?" (James 2:1-4)

All of us should always remember that we cannot serve both God and "mammon." *"No one can serve two masters; for either he will hate the one and love the other, or he will be devoted to one and despise the other. You cannot serve God and wealth."* (Matthew 6:24) (see also Luke 16:13)

CHAPTER FOURTEEN

The Female Wolf – by Cathie Catt

As I have watched my husband, Steven, pour his heart and wisdom into the pages he has written for this book, I have thanked God for what He, through Steven, has been revealing. The Lord has given strong cautions along with strict guidelines so as not to create paranoia in the church. We want to be watchful and aware, but we do not want to cry wolf unnecessarily. The story of the little boy who cried "wolf" is applicable to us today, and this has been clearly presented throughout this book. At last we in the church have practical information on discovering the work of the wolf in the church and what steps we should take to overcome this enemy.

I thought this book was a completed work. However, when our pastor was counseling us about the book he strongly urged that I write a chapter addressing the concept of the female wolf. Although most of the wolf-like traits talked about in the book can apply equally to either a male or female, I believe our pastor is correct. There are certain unique issues concerning female wolves that I believe God has shown me that should be included in this book.

Our pastor's wife also suggested that I address some questions that leaders' wives may face in regard to the female wolf. (I thank her for her input.) I will also attempt to answer some of those questions. So, let's begin.

The scandalous headline may read, "Pastor Caught in Adultery!" How shocking! How devastating to the reputation of the church, to the "man of God," to the character of the Christ that we are supposed to represent! What a blow it is to the morale of the innocent sheep who looked up to and depended upon that pastor. What a heyday it creates for the press, and what ammunition it provides to those who despise the church and all it stands for. And sadly, it is all too often true.

Those of us who have been around the church world for any length of time know all too well the list of famous names that have been brought down this way. Only God knows the list of names of the not-so-famous leaders who likewise have been brought down through adultery. Or perhaps they have successfully hidden it from the church, but God knows their names, too.

What is going on here? How could this possibly happen? Were they ignorant? Haven't these men read the scriptures telling them that adultery is a sin? Well, of course they are not ignorant, and of course they have read the scriptures concerning adultery. But we must never underestimate the subtle craftiness Satan can employ using the female wolf.

The book of Proverbs is chock full of warnings about the harlot or adulteress. God knew what a huge problem this would be so He spared no words in addressing the issue. I will not recount all the verses here, but I want to focus on one verse in Proverbs chapter six. *"For on account of a harlot one is reduced to a loaf of bread, And an adulteress hunts for the precious life."* (Proverbs 6:26)

Look at that again. "…An adulteress *hunts* for the precious life." (emphasis is mine) She hunts! That word "hunt" in the Hebrew is *tsud*, which means to lie in wait, to catch, or to hunt. With the true nature of a wolf, she stalks (lies in wait), hunts, and catches her prey. She is the aggressor; she is the hunter. Her weaponry is effective and covers a wide range of methods. She will use anything from the "damsel in distress" to the seductive temptress to catch her prey. She intends, whatever it takes, to catch the "precious life."

So, just what is the precious life? The word in the Hebrew that is translated "precious" is *yaqar*. It means valuable, costly, rare, or weighty. Looking through the eyes of a wolf, what could be more valuable than the man at the top, the "big cheese," so to speak? There are men in abundance throughout the church, but the men of leadership are rarer by far. They command more authority; they carry the *kabod*, or the weight of glory. In the eyes of a wolf nothing is more precious than the life of the leader.

Let me stop for a moment at this point. It is imperative that I point out that it is not only female wolves who are drawn to the man of God in the leadership position. Consciously or subconsciously, many women are drawn to the authority, the spirit, the gifting of the man of God, and in particular the senior pastor. Some will be immature, innocent sheep who are desperately seeking God and see Christ shining through the pastor. These women want to draw close to the pastor in order to hear from God and find answers they need. They are comforted by the rod and staff the pastor holds. They have no devious motives. They need God and they need their shepherd.

Other women may be more mature in Christ, but perhaps have a troubled home life. Maybe her husband does not serve the Lord. This woman sees the pastor in the pulpit, hears his wisdom, and sees his service to the Lord. She is not close enough to him to see his little weaknesses or other foibles, but only sees the anointing of God on him. In her mind she may wish that her husband were more like the pastor. She may be drawn to that pastor, not realizing that she is only being drawn to a fantasy. She has not seen the cracks in the jar of clay; she only sees the treasure – the sermons, the anointing, and the ministry during the church services. (see 2 Corinthians 4:7)

Regardless of her motivation and whether or not she is a wolf, the results could be the same. Innocent, immature sheep can be manipulated by the enemy and fall victim to temptation. Delusion or deception can cause a mature Christian woman to fall into the same temptation. And the female wolf may go in to the situation with purpose and deliberation. In each case it is up to the shepherd to defend against the possibility of falling into the enemy's trap.

Many practical steps can be taken by the shepherd to guard himself in these cases. 1 Corinthians 6:18 bluntly says, *"Flee immorality. ..."* Flee (*pheugo* in the Greek) means run away, shun, or escape. This is the smartest thing to do. The pastor simply must not put himself in a position where things can get out of hand. He does not want to fall to any sexual lure, nor does he want to find himself caught up in a feeling of rescuing the fair maiden. Our enemy, Satan, is very skillful at manipulating circumstances to take full advantage of any weaknesses a leader may have. The leader must not be ignorant of the enemy's schemes. (see 2 Corinthians 2:11)

Also, the leader must always bear in mind that it is his gift that is drawing the woman. He must not confuse this attraction with that of a more personal nature and let his ego be unduly inflated. If he keeps this in mind, he will more easily view the situation with the objectivity needed to accurately assess the woman's motivation, and he will know what course of action he should follow.

If counseling is needed as in the case of the immature, innocent sheep, the counseling should never be done in an intimate one-on-one basis. It must be done with some other trusted person present, preferably the pastor's wife. This can help establish the idea in the woman's mind of the unity between the pastor and his wife, and at the same time discourage any thoughts that he may be open to anyone else's advances.

If the woman continues beyond a simple need for some counseling, or in any other way becomes more persistent or even aggressive in her pursuit of the pastor, he must again seek out the safety provided by his elders. He must frankly share his concerns with the elders so that nothing remains hidden. (see John 3:19-21) This is another time when the pastor's wife must definitely be "in the loop."

If the woman is just misguided in her longing for the ideal she thinks she sees in the pastor, this may be the time for the pastor's wife or other godly women in the church to guide her into a healthier alternative – fellowship with the other women. Women need relationship, and healthy fellowship among the women of the church should be encouraged and fostered. From these relationships she may find just the support she needs to stand and even grow in her difficult situation. She may find other women who have traveled the path she is on and who can give her encouragement with their own testimonies of how God brought them through. In addition, there are many areas of service in the Kingdom of God that can fill great voids in our lives as well. As she finds her own unique place of service in the body of Christ, the blessing of God will rest on her. Unlike the fantasy the misguided woman may have pursued, these things will genuinely strengthen and mature her.

But what if this is not what she wants? What if she continues to pursue the pastor? This may be a female wolf. Has the woman sent any inappropriate emails, texts, or any other communications to the pastor? These need to be seen and documented by the whole leadership team. They ought to guard against the possibility of any sort of false charges that may be made against the pastor. All it takes is one vindictive woman who feels she has been scorned to raise such an outcry that it could damage the reputation of both the pastor and the church. All of leadership must be united to protect the pastor.

In addition to protecting the pastor, the elders are now alerted to the possibility of a female wolf in the church who may very well divert her attention to a different leader once she finds that the senior pastor is inaccessible. They must be on their guard as well. If the woman is found to truly be a wolf, the steps outlined elsewhere in this book now apply.

"Behold, I send you out as sheep in the midst of wolves; so be shrewd as serpents and innocent as doves." (Matthew 10:16) Leaders must be wise.

A second uniquely female wolf is one that may be described as the "uncovered woman." Although all uncovered women can potentially cause problems in a church, not all uncovered women are wolves. Let's first describe what an uncovered woman is.

"Wives, be subject to your own husbands, as to the Lord. For the husband is the head of the wife, as Christ also is the head of the church, He Himself being the Savior of the body. But as the church is subject to Christ, so also the wives ought to be to their husbands in everything." (Ephesians 5:22-24) An uncovered woman is simply a woman who is not submitted.

Oh, my! What a touchy subject, what a can of worms to be opening up! But open it we must, for it is the Word of God. Even if it is not a popular notion, from this verse and many others we know that the Bible still requires that we submit to one another.

Yes, we are all equal in value in God's sight. There is neither male nor female in Christ. (see Galatians 3:28) But we are the body of Christ, and we can't all be the eye. We are all valuable, but we all have different functions. We have different giftings. We have different spheres of authority. We can't have a renegade hand that won't obey the signals given by the brain. There must be some order and flow for the body to function properly and efficiently. God is a God of order. (see 1 Corinthians 14:33)

If a woman won't submit to her husband, she won't submit to the pastor. If she won't submit to the pastor, ultimately she won't submit to the Lord because it is the Lord who said, "Wives, be subject to your own husbands, *as to the Lord*." (emphasis mine) Women will not be any more submitted to the Lord than they are to their husbands! And I know, I know; I have heard the all the questions about, "What if my husband asks me to … (something outrageous is inserted here, such as go to a strip club)?" Well, chances are that he hasn't ever asked her to go to a strip club (or whatever), and probably never will. On the rare chance that some husband ever does, that wife needs to seek the counsel of the pastor right away. But usually statements such as this are just means of justifying the idea of not having to submit.

I don't want to get bogged down or off on a rabbit trail with the concept of submission, and I certainly know that no husband or leader is perfect, making the correct decision every single time. I also know that we should obey God rather than man. (see Acts 5:29) However, suffice it to say that the concept of submission is clearly defined in the Bible and not just once, but numerous times. We must not neglect this principle. We must submit to those in authority over us. *"Obey your leaders and submit to them, for they **keep watch over your souls** as those who will give an account. Let them do this with joy and not with grief, for this would be unprofitable for you."* (Hebrews 13:17 emphasis is mine) Submission gives us a "covering," someone to watch over our soul. Without submission we are "uncovered."

We now know what an uncovered woman is, so let's begin to look at some of the problems she creates and how to differentiate between a problem sheep and a wolf.

"Now concerning spiritual gifts, brethren, I do not want you to be unaware. ... Now there are varieties of gifts, but the same Spirit. And there are varieties of ministries, and the same Lord. There are varieties of effects, but the same God who works all things in all persons. But to each one is given the manifestation of the Spirit for the common good." (1 Corinthians 12:1, 4-7) God gives different giftings to the members (women included) of the body of Christ as it has seemed good to Him. Each one of us has a built-in yearning to function in our own gift and to know the fulfillment only found in doing God's will. There is no problem with that yearning. There is no problem with the gift; the problem arises with the authority to use or function in the gift.

This is the point where lack of submission comes into play. Simply put, one cannot have authority without being under authority. Let's look at the story of the centurion desiring Jesus to heal his servant found in Matthew chapter eight and Luke chapter seven.

And when Jesus entered Capernaum, a centurion came to Him, imploring Him, and saying, "Lord, my servant is lying paralyzed at home, fearfully tormented." Jesus said to him, "I will come and heal him." But the centurion said, "Lord, I am not worthy for You to come under my roof, but just say the word, and my servant will be healed. For I also am a man **under authority***, with soldiers under me; and I say to this one, 'Go!' and he goes, and to another, 'Come!' and he comes, and to my slave, 'Do this!' and he does it." Now when Jesus heard this, He marveled and said to those who were following, "Truly I say to* *you, I have not found such great faith with anyone in Israel. I say to you that many will come from east and west, and recline at the table with Abraham, Isaac and Jacob in the kingdom of heaven; but the sons of the kingdom will be cast out into the outer darkness; in that place there will be weeping and gnashing of teeth." And Jesus said to the centurion, "Go; it shall be done for you as you have believed." And the servant was healed that very moment.* (Matthew 8:5-13 emphasis added)

The centurion served and was under the authority of the Roman Empire. When he remained in his position as a centurion in that empire, he had the whole authority of the Roman Empire backing him up when he gave commands. He recognized that Jesus was under the authority of the Father in heaven, so when Jesus spoke He had the whole authority of heaven backing him up. The same concept applies to us, when we are *under* authority we *have* authority.

When the uncovered woman (she is not *under* authority) tries to use her gift, she must *usurp* the authority to do so. The Greek word for usurp is *authenteo*, and according to Strong's means to "act of oneself," to "dominate," to "usurp authority over." She "acts of herself," that is on her own authority without God, the church, or anyone else backing her up. The problems that this creates should be obvious, but it doesn't tell us if she is a wolf or not.

If the gifted woman is so overly excited about her gifting that she is trying to use it in an inappropriate manner, she is not a wolf. She just needs instruction. If she is someone who is impatient and not waiting for proper training or for proper sanctioning by the leadership, she is not a wolf. She just needs some correction and discipline. Temperament has a lot to do with these kinds of problems. Women of a headstrong nature sometimes have difficulty waiting for proper channels to open up. But the maturity she gains from learning to wait will enhance the proper functioning of her gift once the endorsement of leadership is given.

Of course, it is up to the leadership to make sure that there is a legitimate place for the various gifts to operate. Gifted people with no outlet for the use of their gift will become very frustrated and may begin to cause all kinds of problems. Wise leaders recognize and make room for all the gifts of God given to the individuals in the church.

Back to the female wolf. The female wolf may very well be gifted, but she is not submitted. Indeed, she does not want to be submitted. She wants to use her gifting to promote her own agenda. She may use that gifting to draw the sheep away from the shepherd and to herself. She may be self-deceived and think that she is doing God a favor with her subversive actions. She may feel she knows more or hears God more clearly than the pastor. But rebellion (and this is rebellion) is never endorsed by God. *"For **rebellion** is as the sin of **witchcraft**, and stubbornness is as iniquity and idolatry. ..."* (1 Samuel 15:23 KJV) This female wolf must be dealt with; Matthew chapter eighteen still applies. (see the chapter on Scripturally Uncovering the Wolf)

Another uncovered woman who may be a female wolf is one that is very insidious indeed. She manipulates and controls from behind the scenes. Sometimes this type of person is referred to as having a "Jezebel spirit." In 1 Kings 16:31 we see where Ahab, the king of Israel, married Jezebel. *"It came about, as though it had been a trivial thing for him [King Ahab] to walk in the sins of Jeroboam the son of Nebat, that he married Jezebel the daughter of Ethbaal king of the Sidonians, and went to serve Baal and worshiped him."* Ahab was the one anointed to be king over Israel. Jezebel had no anointing of her own; she manipulated and controlled things through Ahab, who was the one with an anointing, and through her relationship to him. Every Jezebel needs an Ahab. Every female wolf who works in this manner needs someone with the anointing through whom she can manipulate and control.

Obviously, most pastors are not at all like the wicked King Ahab. They do not deliberately make alliances with anyone who can pervert or lead them or the church astray. And since this is the case, this female wolf must be very clever in her way of gaining access to and the confidence of the leadership. She must not go around throwing up a lot of red flags. She must come in subtly, and many times she will come in through the "back door."

What do I mean by saying, "coming in through the back door?" I mean that instead of approaching the leader directly, she will begin to try to ingratiate herself to the pastor or leader's family. She may approach and try to "befriend" the pastor's wife. She may lavish attention and gifts on the pastor's children. She may appear as the nurturing, grandmotherly type who just loves the children, eagerly offering to watch and care for them so the pastor's wife can run some errands. In fact, she may appear as a wonderful answer to a busy pastor's wife's prayer.

So how can the leader's wife tell if this is a female wolf or an answer to prayer? We don't want to become jaded and mistrustful of everyone. We don't want to cry "wolf" at the first sign we see of anyone trying to get close to us. But on the other hand, we don't want to be naïve and just take all things at face value. *"The prudent sees the evil and hides himself, But the naive go on, and are punished for it."* (Proverbs 22:3) We will suffer the consequences if we are not prudent. As stated before in this book, it is better to be wary than to be caught unaware.

The first thing to look at is whether or not this woman is submitted to her own husband. If she is not, she is not the kind of person to be intimately associated with the pastor's family even if she is not a wolf. As described above, she is working without the safety of her husband's (and pastor's) covering. A covering guards us and gives us a spiritual protection; without it we are in a dangerous place. Without a covering it is possible to be caught in the devil's snare and to be found doing his will. *"...and they may come to their senses and escape from the **snare of the devil**, having been held captive by him to **do his will**."* (2 Timothy 2:26 emphasis added)

At the very least, this lack of submission presents a very bad example for the children. In this present culture where children are encouraged to be self-assertive, we don't want to seem to be giving our approval to a person who is independent and unsubmitted. When an uncovered woman is accepted into intimate relationship with the family, it only adds to the lure of becoming self-assertive for the children. Children need no help in wanting what they want. They need help and training in giving themselves to the will of God rather than their own will. We do not want *self* to be asserted; we want *Christ* to be seen in us.

> *"But realize this, that in the last days difficult times will come. For men will be **lovers of self**, lovers of money, boastful, arrogant, revilers, disobedient to parents, ungrateful, unholy, unloving, irreconcilable, malicious gossips, without self-control, brutal, haters of good, treacherous, reckless, conceited, lovers of pleasure rather than lovers of God, holding to a form of godliness, although they have denied its power; Avoid such men as these."* (2 Timothy 3:1-5 emphasis added)

Apart from looking at the woman's submission level, the leader's wife would be wise to "test the woman's spirit." *"Beloved, do not believe every spirit, but test the spirits to see whether they are from God, because many false prophets have gone out into the world."* (1 John 4:1) This female wolf may not be a prophet, but as she attempts to connect herself to a "prophet" (that is, someone with an anointing) to accomplish her own agenda, her character, her motives, and her spirit must be examined. Some have felt that women are more naturally discerning and intuitive in examining the motives of others, but I have not found it to necessarily be so. It seems to be more connected to an individual's gifting than anything else. If the leader's wife is gifted with discerning of spirits (see 1 Corinthians 12:10) the job of testing the woman's spirit will be a lot easier. But if that is not her gift, if she is by nature very open and trusting, this can become very problematic. As I said before, we do not want to become jaded and mistrustful of everyone we meet, so what safety measures can we take? The answer lies in the multifaceted or manifold grace of God.

*"As each one has received a special gift, employ it in serving one another as good stewards of the **manifold grace** of God."* (1 Peter 4:10 emphasis added) We all have different giftings; we are the body of Christ. God has designed us to *need* one another.

> *"For the body is not one member, but many. If the foot says, 'Because I am not a hand, I am not a part of the body,' it is not for this reason any the less a part of the body. And if the ear says, 'Because I am not an eye, I am not a part of the body,' it is not for this reason any the less a part of the body. If the whole body were an eye, where would the hearing be? If the whole were hearing, where would the sense of smell be? But now God has placed the members, each one of them, in the body, just as He desired. If they were all one member, where would the body be? But now there are many members, but one body.*

And the eye cannot say to the hand, 'I have no need of you'; or again the head to the feet, 'I have no need of you.' On the contrary, it is much truer that the members of the body which seem to be weaker are necessary; and those members of the body which we deem less honorable, on these we bestow more abundant honor, and our less presentable members become much more presentable, whereas our more presentable members have no need of it. But God has so composed the body, giving more abundant honor to that member which lacked, so that there may be no division in the body, but that the members may have the same care for one another." (1 Corinthians 12:14-25)

Does the leader's wife have a friend or friends with other giftings whom she can trust to help her discern the truth? All leaders' wives should develop a circle of trusted friends who can "shore up" their own weak places. As we develop these relationships, we can safely rely on the working of God in one another. Then we are strengthened through the input of God through others. (see Ephesians 4:16)

And of course, the one voice the wife should be able to trust in these kinds of matters is her husband's. Although she may be reluctant to burden him, especially if he is very busy with all the responsibilities of his work in the church, ultimately, God holds the husband responsible for the care of his family. Just as Adam was charged with caring for the garden and keeping the serpent out, husbands should be caring for and guarding their own "gardens." Any leader that is too busy to watch over his own family is too busy. Something is out of balance somewhere. (see Ephesians 5:25)

But whether or not this manipulative female wolf comes in the back door or by a more direct route, vigilance and steadfast watchfulness are always needed. Thank God for strong leadership!

We really are as sheep among wolves (see Matthew 10:16). So whatever wolf we face, we should remember that we have not been abandoned. *"… I will never desert you, nor will I ever forsake you."* (Hebrews 13:5) Our Shepherd is always with us (read the 23rd Psalm). He has not sent us to fail or be defeated. He has called and equipped us to be victorious, in fact we are more than conquerors! *"Who will separate us from the love of Christ? Will tribulation, or distress, or persecution, or famine, or nakedness, or peril, or sword? Just as it is written, 'For your sake we are being put to death all day long; we were considered as sheep to be slaughtered.' But in all these things **we overwhelmingly conquer through Him** who loved us. For I am convinced that neither death, nor life, nor angels, nor principalities, nor things present, nor things to come, nor powers, nor height, nor depth, nor any other created thing, will be able to separate us from the love of God, which is in Christ Jesus our Lord."* (Romans 8:35-39 emphasis added)

I pray that leaders would begin to go conquer the wolf because Jesus paid a high price for His sheep!

CHAPTER FIFTEEN

The Wolves Want your Vineyard (Jezebel and Ahab)

In the previous chapter Cathie wrote about the female wolf and referenced Jezebel and her controlling spirit. Let's go a little farther with this and deal with the next aspect of Jezebel which is conspiracy and agreement. I think we all know the story of Naboth, his vineyard, and how Jezebel conspired against Naboth, had him killed, and took his vineyard. But, let's look at the story from scripture:

"Now it came about after these things that Naboth the Jezreelite had a vineyard which was in Jezreel beside the palace of Ahab king of Samaria. Ahab spoke to Naboth, saying, 'Give me your vineyard, that I may have it for a vegetable garden because it is close beside my house, and I will give you a better vineyard than it in its place; if you like, I will give you the price of it in money.' But Naboth said to Ahab, 'The LORD forbid me that I should give you the inheritance of my fathers.' So Ahab came into his house sullen and vexed because of the word which Naboth the Jezreelite had spoken to him; for he said, 'I will

*not give you the inheritance of my fathers.' And he lay down on his bed and turned away his face and ate no food. But Jezebel his wife came to him and said to him, 'How is it that your spirit is so sullen that you are not eating food?' So he said to her, 'Because I spoke to Naboth the Jezreelite and said to him, "Give me your vineyard for money; or else, if it pleases you, I will give you a vineyard in its place." But he said, "I will not give you my vineyard."' Jezebel his wife said to him, 'Do you now reign over Israel? Arise, eat bread, and let your heart be joyful; **I will give you the vineyard of Naboth the Jezreelite.**' So she wrote letters in Ahab's name and sealed them with his seal, and sent letters to the elders and to the nobles who were living with Naboth in his city. Now she wrote in the letters, saying, 'Proclaim a fast and seat Naboth at the head of the people; and seat two worthless men before him, and let them testify against him, saying, "You cursed God and the king." Then take him out and stone him to death.' So the men of his city, the elders and the nobles who lived in his city, did as Jezebel had sent word to them, just as it was written in the letters which she had sent them. They proclaimed a fast and seated Naboth at the head of the people. Then the two worthless men came in and sat before him; and the worthless men testified against him, even against Naboth, before the people, saying, 'Naboth cursed God and the king.' So they took him outside the city and stoned him to death with stones. Then they sent word to Jezebel, saying, 'Naboth has been stoned and is dead.' When Jezebel heard that Naboth had been stoned and was dead, Jezebel said to Ahab, 'Arise, take possession of the vineyard of Naboth, the Jezreelite, which he refused to give you for money; for Naboth is not alive,* *but dead.' When Ahab heard that Naboth was dead, Ahab arose to go down to the vineyard of Naboth the Jezreelite, to take possession of it."* (1 Kings 21:1-16 emphasis added)

My cousin, Michele Perry, who has a strong prophetic ministry, recently made a statement to me that spoke volumes. She said, "Every Jezebel needs an Ahab." Jezebel does not work alone! She needs someone who will come into agreement with her and give her authority to act, backing her every decision.

Notice how Jezebel promised Ahab, "*I* will give you the vineyard." At no point did Ahab ask, "How?" or "Wait a minute, what are you up to?" Ahab wasn't concerned with how she was going to do it; he just wanted that vineyard. By his *silence* Ahab came into *agreement* with her and gave her permission to go ahead with her plan. Leaders must be very careful that by their silence they are not giving permission to someone with evil intentions. It is time for true leadership to break the silence and speak up. Go ahead, leaders, give a clear warning.

*"Cry loudly, do not hold back; **Raise your voice like a trumpet**, And declare to My people their transgression And to the house of Jacob their sins."* (Isaiah 58:1 emphasis added)

I recently got word of a hostile takeover of a thriving, established church in a nearby state. This is not surprising news to me anymore because I hear of these ungodly takeovers on a regular basis. A very ambitious husband and wife ministry team came into a large city and set their sights on another man's church. Because this couple had ministered in that city many times before, they had made many relationships with a number of churches in that region. Somewhere along the way a conversation between this visiting ministry team and another couple took place. It only took one person to say, "I wish you would come and pastor our church," for the idea of a takeover to be planted. The wife of the visiting minister, being the stronger personality of the two, immediately began to orchestrate a plan to take that church which was currently being pastored by a loving, older pastor. Because the pastor was aging, the story was spread that he was no longer capable of leading the church and that a younger, more powerful voice was needed. Once the story was started, the people took it from there. A meeting to discuss the pastor's future was held, and the pastor was sent away, devastated and broken-hearted. The younger couple took charge of the church with no apparent regret for what they had done.

This event reminded me of the story that we just read in I Kings where Naboth had a vineyard that was of great value to him. I see Naboth as the pastor and his vineyard (that which bears fruit) as his church. I see King Ahab as the unethical young man eyeing another man's church or "vineyard," if you will, and his wife as Jezebel, his accomplice.

The one thing that sent a shiver down my back was the fact that having Naboth killed meant nothing to Jezebel as long as she got what she wanted. In that same spirit, this Ahab and Jezebel type couple destroyed an older pastor's remaining years, took his church, and showed absolutely no remorse for their actions. I wonder how many other wolves named Ahab and Jezebel are out there right now coming into agreement to take another man's vineyard?

CHAPTER SIXTEEN

Scripturally Uncovering the Wolf

Hopefully by now the leaders have done all that they can to protect their "flock." They have strengthened the weak places in the fence; they have taken the rebellious sheep to the gate and turned them loose. The leaders have acquainted themselves with the wolf's hunting strategy and with the wolf's tactics and traits. The leaders have examined the footprints, and they have discovered a wolf in sheep's clothing in their church. Now they must act. How do they uncover that wolf?

"If your brother sins, go and show him his fault in private; if he listens to you, you have won your brother. But if he does not listen to you, take one or two more with you, so that by the mouth of two or three witnesses every fact may be confirmed. If he refuses to listen to them, tell it to the church; and if he refuses to listen even to the church, let him be to you as a Gentile and a tax collector." (Matthew 18:15-17) The scripture is clear, but there are a few things the senior pastor should attend to before confronting the wolf.

First, the senior pastor must take his elders into his confidence. He should let them know what he is seeing and what he is concerned about. The senior pastor should ask them if they are seeing or sensing anything as well. He should be willing to hear their input. *"… wisdom is with those who receive counsel."* (Proverbs 13:10) Leaders must remember that they are all in this thing together.

Secondly, the pastor should confront the suspected wolf face to face alone. But the wise leader will make sure that he is strong in the Lord before having this face to face talk with the individual in question. He should never enter confrontation without prayer and fasting.

When confronting the person the leader must stick to the facts. It is important at this time that the pastor deal only with the things that he knows to be true. He should avoid being arrogant or angry because these are not evidences of Christ's character in him. The leader should let the wolf see his anointing and his godly character, not his flesh.

This is also the time when he will observe how the person reacts to confrontation to either confirm his suspicions or put them to rest. (refer to the last paragraph of the Introduction) The leader should always look for signs of repentance because even with the wolf, the restoration of any soul is the goal. But, I will talk more about the wolf and repentance in a later chapter.

If there is still no repentance, the third thing the pastor must do is to confront the wolf with the elders present. At this point of confrontation with the wolf it is wise to have the strength of a *unified* leadership team. Not only does it conform to the standard given to us in Matthew 18, but it gives protection to the shepherd. We lose too many shepherds to the wolves because they had no one to stand with them. That is one reason why God placed the elders in the church. I encourage pastors to create a strong relationship with their elders before they need their elders' help in matters of this sort.

When the wolf sees the leadership's unity, he realizes that the pastor is not standing alone in this situation. The wolf needs to see the pastor and his elders standing together in unity. He cannot easily break a three-fold cord. (see Ecclesiastes 4:12) It is at this time that the leadership team alerts the wolf that he is one step away from being removed from the church.

If the person still refuses to yield, the last thing that must be done is to reveal the wolf to the church publicly. This is a tough one, but scripture is crystal clear. I have watched many pastors fail to carry out this last step thereby leaving the wolf to continue to walk freely among the sheep. Once the wolf determines that he will not be dealt with, he will once again begin his process of deceiving the sheep. It is true, deal with him now or deal with him later, but sooner or later leaders will have to deal with the wolf.

CHAPTER SEVENTEEN

Repentant Wolf?

I must now address a very serious and important question. It is one that in all my studies on uncovering wolves I had never even given any thought to until a pastor asked me, "Can a wolf ever change?" In the natural we know that this is an impossibility. But what about in the spiritual? What about the wolf and repentance? Fortunately, the things that are impossible in the natural are possible with God. *"And looking at them Jesus said to them, 'With people this is impossible, but **with God all things are possible.**'"* (Matthew 19:26 emphasis added) (also see Mark 10:27)

Let's look for a moment at Saul of Tarsus. Was Saul a wolf? He certainly killed his share of believers. He fought the gospel of Christ. He fostered hatred of Christians. He was there when Stephen was stoned and did nothing to stop it. (see Acts 7:58, 8:1 & 3, 9:1-2) He was truly behaving like a wolf, ravaging the church.

But in spite of all that Saul had done, there came a moment in his life when he had an encounter with the Lord. *"Now Saul, still breathing threats and murder against the disciples of the Lord, went to the high priest, and asked for letters from him to the synagogues at Damascus, so that if he found any belonging to the Way, both men and women, he might bring them bound to Jerusalem. As he was traveling, it happened that he was approaching Damascus, and suddenly a light from heaven flashed around him; and he fell to the ground and heard a voice saying to him, 'Saul, Saul, why are you persecuting Me?' And he said, 'Who are You, Lord?' And He said, 'I am Jesus whom you are persecuting."* (Acts 9:1-5)

Yes, I believe God can bring the wolf to his knees and turn his heart of anger into that of, as in the case of Saul of Tarsus, the loving apostle Paul. God does not want anyone to perish. His heart is always for repentance and restoration. *"The Lord is not slow about His promise, as some count slowness, but is patient toward you, **not wishing for any to perish but for all to come to repentance."*** (2 Peter 3:9 emphasis added)

That should be our attitude as well. I am so grateful for His longsuffering and forgiving love. If anyone is to be Christ-like he must also develop a longsuffering nature. We should all remember that there was a time when each of us needed His forgiveness. Sometimes someone in our lives needs our forgiveness as well.

Knowing all of this, leaders must judge the wolf with a shepherd's heart. Repentance and restoration should always be the goal. All life is precious, even that of the wolf, and I take no joy in seeing anyone destroyed. In fact, the Bible clearly says to take no joy when an enemy falls. *"Do not rejoice when your enemy falls, And do not let your heart be glad when he stumbles."* (Proverbs 24:17) I want to encourage every leader to go into each situation with godliness, justice, and restoration in his heart.

In the case of Saul, who obviously was at war with the church, God spoke to a man named Ananias. He told Ananias to go pray for Saul. To which Ananias replied, "But, God, Saul is our enemy!"

*"Now there was a disciple at Damascus named
Ananias; and the Lord said to him in a vision,
'Ananias.' And he said, 'Here I am, Lord.' And the
Lord said to him, 'Get up and go to the street called
Straight, and inquire at the house of Judas for a man
from Tarsus named Saul, for he is praying, and he
has seen in a vision a man named Ananias come in
and lay his hands on him, so that he might regain
his sight.' But Ananias answered, 'Lord, I have
heard from many about this man, how much harm
he did to Your saints at Jerusalem; and here he has
authority from the chief priests to bind all who call
on Your name.' But the Lord said to him, 'Go, for
he is a chosen instrument of Mine, to bear My name
before the Gentiles and kings and the sons of Israel;
for I will show him how much he must suffer for
My name's sake.' So Ananias departed and entered
the house, and after laying his hands on him said,
'Brother Saul, the Lord Jesus, who appeared to you
on the road by which you were coming, has sent me
so that you may regain your sight and be filled with
the Holy Spirit.'"* (Acts 9:10-17)

Ananias said, "Lord, I have heard from many concerning
this man, and how much harm he has done to the saints at
Jerusalem." Have you ever questioned someone's conver-
sion because they had done so much damage? That may be a
very natural reaction. But, in the case of Saul of Tarsus, God
was very clear when He said, "He is a chosen instrument
of Mine." Ananias was obedient to God, and went to pray
for Saul. He even addressed him as "Brother Saul." God's
mercy and forgiveness are real.

In keeping with this same theme there is another touching
story I want to look at. But this one is not only one of forgiveness but of restoration as well. It's found in the story of the

prodigal son. I can sum this young man's turbulent life up in a few short terms. He had it all … He demanded it all … He wasted it all … He lost it all … And he got it all back! We all know the story. We see a repentant young man who represents mankind and the willing, forgiving father who represents God.

But what I want us to focus our eyes on is the older brother. The younger son is restored, the father is thrilled, but what is happening in the heart of that older son? Scripture says that in the midst all of the celebration the older sibling is angry!

*"Now his older son was in the field, and when he came and approached the house, he heard music and dancing. And he summoned one of the servants and began inquiring what these things could be. And he said to him, 'Your brother has come, and your father has killed the fattened calf because he has received him back safe and sound.' But **he became angry** and was not willing to go in; and his father came out and began pleading with him. But he answered and said to his father, 'Look! For so many years I have been serving you and I have never neglected a command of yours; and yet you have never given me a young goat, so that I might celebrate with my friends; but when this son of yours came, who has devoured your wealth with prostitutes, you killed the fattened calf for him.'"* (Luke 15:25-30 emphasis added)

With all of my heart I believe that the older brother represents the all too familiar attitude of the carnal Christian. I hear it all the time, "Steven, I was faithful. I stayed home. I didn't sin. And yet, the so-called repentant failure gets all of the attention." What do we do when God forgives someone that we think should have been judged? How do we feel when God reclaims even that fallen super star?

Let's make it even more painful. How do *you* feel when God takes the fallen ones, forgives them, restores them, and then "blesses" them? Wait a minute, God! I was faithful.

I stayed home. I worked the field. I carried out Your will at a tremendous emotional cost to myself and my family. God, I am in a day-to-day struggle to make it, and You pour out a blessing on some failed loser who has stumbled back home?

I don't recall a single time when God came to me and said, "Steven, I'm going to forgive so-and-so. What do you think?" I don't want to walk in fear like Ananias and say, "But God, he's a dangerous man." I certainly don't want to take on the attitude of the older brother and whine when God blesses the prodigal. Jesus explained it all when he said, *"Blessed are the merciful, for they shall obtain mercy."* (Matthew 5:7 KJV) Trust me, I can use all of the mercy I can get! I'll tell you the truth; when someone who has failed or wasted the gift makes it back, it fills my eyes with tears.

The leadership team must be the first to show the way in accepting and restoring the repentant wolf. I don't fully understand God's loving, forgiving ways. But I am so glad that He is who He is.

CHAPTER EIGHTEEN

Nehemiah's Wolves

To reinforce this whole study, let's look to an example found in the Bible. Nehemiah, son of Hacaliah, was called by God to restore the walls of the fallen city of Jerusalem. Nehemiah faced three wolves of his own as he labored to restore the burnt and broken ruins of what was once a great city. The enemy had no intentions of allowing the restoration without creating opposition to it. We can glean some insight by examining the wolves Nehemiah faced.

> *"But when Sanballat the Horonite and Tobiah the Ammonite official, and Geshem the Arab heard it, they mocked us and despised us and said, 'What is this thing you are doing? Are you rebelling against the king?'"* (Nehemiah 2:19)

I want to begin with Geshem, the Arab. He was naturally an enemy. I can understand Geshem fighting the restoration because he was an Arab, and he had no love for Jerusalem or its people. In the same manner there are those in the world who have no love for the things of God or the health of the church. They are the "natural enemies."

A prime example of a natural enemy would be atheists. They say, "There is no God." (see Psalms 14:1) Why would they support the work of God? I expect the world to fight the work of God because they have no fellowship with Him. I am never surprised when the world acts like the world.

Secondly, we see the traitor, Tobiah. History tells us that Tobiah's father was in Jerusalem at the time of its fall, but was not willing to fight. So he fled to the land of the Ammonite, and Tobiah was raised there. Tobiah was a Jew by birth, but an Ammonite in his heart. Tobiah represents the wolf who was once in the church, but left. Now he has come back to criticize everything done there.

Tobiah is the one who *should* know what the church is all about, but he has been in a "strange land" long enough that he has developed a foreign philosophy. Tobiah no longer walks in the spirit; he walks in the flesh. He has developed a worldly, critical heart. Tobiah will be missed, but he must go.

The third wolf Nehemiah faced was Sanballat. He was an officer in the court of Artaxerxes, the king. It is inconceivable to me to think that Sanballat did not know of the king's proclamation to Nehemiah to rebuild the walls of Jerusalem. (see Nehemiah 2:5-10) However, even though Sanballat was displeased, he did not argue with the king. He fought the restoration (God's plan) by discouraging the people the king had sent.

Much like Sanballat, the wolf inside the church knows the leader's heart and knows the vision of the church. Sometimes he is even one of the closest people to the senior pastor. But when he is displeased, he is not going to argue with the leader. There is no future in that! He is going to seek to discourage the workers under the leader. At no point did Sanballat argue with King Artaxerses over the restoration of Jerusalem. And so also the Sanballat type wolf will not argue with the senior pastor. He will go directly to Nehemiah (the one responsible for carrying out the plan).

For example, if the wolf has a disagreement with the pastor over the direction of the youth program, more than likely he will not argue with the pastor. He will go directly to the youth leader and sow his discord there. This wolf can be extremely disruptive because there is a sense that there is a problem in the church, but it can't seem to be pinpointed.

This wolf bypasses authority and creates confusion. The wolf dare not show himself to the shepherd because that would mean his immediate death. So he quietly works to hinder the restoration by sowing discouragement among the workers. This wolf is not working under cover. He is simply staying out of the shepherd's view. He is depending on little or no communication among leaders so that he can continue to fight the vision just out of the pastor's sight.

However, if the people working with the pastor are truly joined to the pastor, they will reveal the wolf's intentions. Young leaders must be taught to run to the senior pastor if they suspect the wolf is near. I know that I have said it before, but I will say it again: It is better to be cautious than to be caught unaware. Remember in John 10:3-5 it says that sheep know their shepherd's voice and will not follow a stranger's voice. If there is a young leader who is constantly listening to other voices, he must be corrected now before the wolf can turn him against the shepherd.

Nehemiah overcame his wolves and finished his assignment. So can we, if we follow the word of God. The church is not a "self-guided tour." I can't even begin to tell you how many churches I have seen destroyed because they simply didn't go to the Word of God for instruction. For any problem faced, the Word of God has an answer. All too often spiritual matters are dealt with in an angry, carnal fashion which never produces godly results. And the senior pastor should remember God has given him elders as a safety net. He shouldn't jump without his elders in place.

CHAPTER NINETEEN

Communicating Shepherd to Shepherd

If someone comes from another local church and there is any question as to their intentions, the leadership should not hesitate to call the former pastor and inquire as to why that person left his church and has come to them. That way it can be determined early if this is a roving wolf or simply a sheep out of pocket.

It is imperative at this point that leaders be honest with each other about the problems they have had with a person, but they must be sure that their anger doesn't get in the way of the whole truth and nothing but the truth. *"... But everyone must be quick to hear, slow to speak and slow to anger; for the anger of man does not achieve the righteousness of God."* (James 1:19-20)

Let me stress this most important point at this time: All conversations between pastors regarding another church's problems or sheep need to be kept in the strictest of confidence! There are warnings that are for the leaders' ears *only* and not to be shared publicly. Some things even their spouses do not need to hear about. However, if the spouse is privy to certain things, it goes without saying that these things should not be discussed anywhere with anyone. We are not here to gossip about or brand anyone as a troublemaker until all facts are brought to light. In fact, I have witnessed people who were branded as wolves and troublemakers in one church that landed in another church where they subsequently functioned without problems of any kind. They were simply sheep in the wrong church. *"But now God has placed the members, each one of them, in the body, just as He desired."* (1 Corinthians 12:18) We can flourish if we allow God to place us in the proper position (the correct sheepfold, if you will) in the body of Christ.

And let's face it, not all pastors are easy to get along with. I've got to tell you, some preachers just grind my nerves. I could not easily sit under their ministry. I am sure that there are those who would find it difficult to be joined with me in ministry. This is nothing more than a simple personality conflict. The body of Christ is vast; there is a place for everyone to be "fitly joined" together.

Another reason sheep may have difficulty flourishing under a particular ministry is because of the leader's personal wounds. Wounded leaders may lash out at the sheep when it is not necessary. I know of one pastor who, because of a wound from his past, would regularly beat the sheep if he thought they were coming too near his wound.

If we take a lesson from the Old Testament, we can see that when the warriors were circumcised God warned the leadership not to allow those soldiers to leave the camp and join battle until they had completely healed. (see Joshua 5:8) When the wounded shepherd preaches, he "bleeds" on the sheep. That does nothing to heal the wounds of the people. In fact, wounded shepherds may find it necessary to stay out of the pulpit until they deal with the things that are dealing with them. Keep in mind that it is not the leader's blood on the sheep that cleanses, but only Jesus' blood.

A third reason some people may not fit in is nothing more than "growing pains." They are simply adolescent sheep. Let's face it, adolescent sheep think they know everything, and they will tell everyone so. Much like dealing with teenagers, some things only come with time and maturity. Leaders don't want to destroy the adolescent sheep, and they certainly don't want to unjustly brand someone as a wolf for life.

A verbal "tar and feathering" can be painful, and words and labels can stick forever. So it is extremely important to be very, very careful when "crying wolf." That term may very well scar someone for life.

Now I know that it can hurt when a shepherd loses a sheep. But the truth of the matter is that not everyone who starts with a local church will stay with that church. Just because someone leaves a particular church it doesn't mean that he cannot flourish somewhere else.

This brings up the question: What should the leadership do if someone in their church is not "fitly joined?" Perhaps the leadership could encourage the individual to visit around and find a place where he or she can become a part. If the leadership is truly concerned about that person's spiritual well-being, they will want to see him planted where he can grow. In fact, they could offer to call other pastors to say that they were sending someone on with their blessing.

The pastor and elders shouldn't take it personally if someone leaves them and is blessed in another church. If that person had stayed, it would only have been continuing tension. And more tension is not something any church needs. Sometimes people simply need help finding a home.

CHAPTER TWENTY

Forming a Network of Watchmen in the City

(Ezekiel 33:1-6 emphasis added) *"And the word of the LORD came to me, saying, 'Son of man, speak to the sons of your people and say to them, If I bring a sword upon a land, and the people of the land take one man from among them and **make him their watchman**, and he sees the sword coming upon the land and blows on the trumpet and warns the people, then he who hears the sound of the trumpet and does not take warning, and a sword comes and takes him away, his blood will be on his own head. He heard the sound of the trumpet but did not take warning; his blood will be on himself. But had he taken warning, he would have delivered his life. But if the watchman sees the sword coming and does not blow the trumpet and the people are not warned, and a sword comes and takes a person from them, he is taken away in his iniquity; but his blood I will require from the watchman's hand.'"*

L eaders are the watchmen over the city. God strategically places ministries and watchmen throughout the region in order to protect the sheep from enemies that would attempt to approach undetected. Some are in the east and others in the west. From the street mission downtown to the affluent church in the suburbs, God has placed watchmen throughout the region. Can you imagine the security this would create if ministers would drop their differences and communicate from one corner of the city to another? The wolf would find it difficult to operate in a city that had the watchmen in place.

There is so much synergy in united leadership. United shepherds not only protect their churches from the wolf, but the rest of the city as well! Drugs, gangs, school shootings, and domestic violence will continue to increase until the shepherds in that city unite in prayer and stand side by side. Leaders must stop comparing doctrine and start proclaiming, "Restoration in this city." They should stop looking at their local church as *the* "House of God," and start looking at their city, their nation, their world as the "House of God." Then they can begin expanding their protection and influence to a region not just a building. I have met pastors who have great influence on the city council and in the community as a whole. Thank God! They are beginning to build a spiritual covering for the entire city.

Let me assure you that the verse of scripture is true when Jesus said, "A house divided against itself cannot stand." (see Matthew 12:25, Mark 3:25, and Luke 11:17) If unity is required in the congregation, it ought to be required of godly leaders as well. If leaders will stand together against the real enemy, they can raise up a spiritual hedge of protection. In short, leaders can stand together or fall separately. The choice is theirs.

By standing together, shepherds in a region can develop a "network of trust" and form an "early warning system."

They truly become biblical watchmen as well as a spiritual covering.

One aspect of the covering provided by the gathering together of shepherds is covering the city with corporate prayer. I will illustrate this point with the following example:

In 2007 I brought a prophetic word to a pastor and his church in southwest Texas. The word was, "The city will come to your doorstep not many days from now asking for your help." A few months after the word was given, that the pastor responded to a knock on his door. There stood the chief of police. The chief was asking for this pastor to gather as many other pastors as he could for a special meeting. Pastors from all over the city gathered together as requested, and the chief made this statement, "You, as pastors, are the voice of authority in this city, and we need your help." Crime had increased to the point that, per capita, this small Texas town had more crime than Houston! The chief of police was asking if the leaders could begin to cover the city with prayer. Pastors and their sheep began to walk their city and silently pray. Street by street, they began to wage war in prayer. In a matter of months, crime was on the decrease. But as with so many things the church starts, people lost interest in the project. The number of those walking and praying dwindled. As a result, crime immediately began to increase again. As of late 2008, prayer for their city has found new life and begun again. Once again, crime is going down. The message here is simple, "Pastors, unite together and pray for your city."

In conclusion, any book such as this can never replace prayer and the Word of God. This is only a starting place for your own personal studies. I encourage all who read this to never take someone else's words and receive them as flawless or somehow divine. This is only my study and my heart.

END NOTE

* The term "senior pastor" has been used in this book for simplicity's sake, but I recognize that the senior leader may have some other gifting other than that of pastor.

ACKNOWLEDGMENTS

I am a speaker, not a writer. Therefore this arduous process of writing has been a long and difficult task for me. I never thought this torture would end! I am not computer friendly, either. Seizing upon this weakness in me, my enemy, the computer, has tried many times to steal my sanity. I am proud to report that with lots of help, I have finally survived. My sanity, however, is still in question. (And for you technology lovers out there I must report that no computers were harmed in the writing of this book.)

But, as I stated, this has been a very trying process for me and I want to thank those who have helped me complete this work. I want to give a special thanks to pastor Rigo Magana of New Hope Christian Fellowship in Greeley, CO for first encouraging me by the word of the Lord to put into print the things that God had given me.

Pastor Jim Fogarty of Oasis Foursquare Church in Sierra Vista, AZ took my sermon notes and created my first teaching manual for me. From there I have been able to "flesh out" that "skeleton" and write this book. Thanks!

I am so grateful to Dr. Peter Wyns of Christians for Messiah Ministries for giving me invaluable editing advice and for encouraging me to finish the work.

Those who gave me sound advice by telling me to apply for a copyright were truly sent by God. Thanks, Bishop Phil

Tutor of New Life City Church, Safford, AZ and Chaplain Claude Walker of Crossroads Ministries, Sierra Vista, AZ. I know others also told me to get a copyright, too, but it is hard to name everybody.

I need to mention some of the names of those who have had great input into my life and have given me concepts and ideas that have found their way into this book: my brother, David Catt, and his wife, Valerie, who now live in Florence, CO; Louis Bartet, pastor of Point Assembly of God, Downsville, LA; our friends, Earl and Jane Bennett, also from Point Assembly of God; Marta Smith, the pastor's wife at Ingleside Assembly of God, Ingleside, TX; Evangelist Troy Drake from Paris, TX; Ronny Robinson who is an outreach pastor in Kingsville, TX; Anita Jordan from Downsville, LA; and Dan Jones who was my pastor when I was young, along with his wife, Linda.

I give special thanks, also, to my cousin, Michele Perry of Mountainair, New Mexico, for her section on Jezebel.

I also need to give a special thanks to Janet Rauch of McComb, IL. She has given up many hours of sleep in order to talk to me on the phone and allow me to bounce ideas off of her. She, along with her late husband, Les, has been a great friend of ours throughout our ministry.

Last, I would like to thank my pastor, Bil Cornelius of Bay Area Fellowship, Corpus Christi, TX for encouraging me to get this book published. It was just the push I needed to proceed to the next step God had in mind for me. I am also grateful for his taking the time to write the forward for this book. What an honor!

Praise the LORD! Praise the LORD, O my soul! I will praise the LORD while I live; I will sing praises to my God while I have my being. (Psalms 146:1-2)

ABOUT THE AUTHOR

Steven began his service to the Lord by being faithful in his local church in Lakewood, Colorado where he grew up. He became leader of a successful youth group in the local church, served a term as deacon, and lead the singing for the church. God called Steven into full time ministry in the mid 1970's. So, along with his wife, Cathie, and (at that time) two sons, he sold his house and began traveling in a small motorhome across the United States preaching and singing in various churches.

Throughout his years of ministry, he sang front music for J.D. Sumner and the Stamps Quartet when they appeared in Denver, CO. He has appeared with Warren Black for the 700 Club and has also made a live appearance on TBN in Santa Ana, CA with Dwight Thompson. But most of his ministry has been spent in local churches.

He has taught many marriage seminars as well as bringing a "rhema" word to the body of Christ in the local setting. He has been called to many troubled churches to help them work through their difficulties and to see the will of God carried out in these situations.

Steven's experience dealing with troubled churches over the years has given him a wealth of wisdom on this subject. Recently God has called him to compile some of this wisdom into a book. "When Do I Cry 'Wolf'?" is a valuable tool in identifying and uncovering the deceptive work of the enemy within the church.

God has given Steven a heart for the local church, and in particular for the local leadership. One of his great desires is to assist churches in restructuring their government to achieve a more Biblical structure. This Biblical structure will give them the ability to function properly so that they might fulfill their God-given purpose for their area.

Steven also has a great desire to see people find their place in the body of Christ. He has assisted pastors to identify the giftings in the people of God and to help place them in the right area of service to the Lord.

He and his wife, Cathie, were married in 1969. Together they have three sons and one granddaughter. Currently they live in Corpus Christi, Texas.

Printed in the United States
135808LV00002B/1/P

9 781607 911944